TAKE OFF
YOUR PANTS!

Outline Your Books
for Faster, Better Writing

Libbie Hawker

Take Off Your Pants!

Outline Your Books for Faster, Better Writing

Copyright 2015—Libbie Hawker

Running Rabbit Press

San Juan County, WA

Second Ebook Edition

290 ½

CONTENTS

TAKE OFF
YOUR PANTS!

Outline Your Books
for Faster, Better Writing

The Power of Confidence

January 15th, 2015 was a big day for me. I'd just accepted an offer from Lake Union Publishing—my second book deal with my publisher. A few weeks before, I'd sent them a proposal for a new historical novel, along with a rough draft of the first few chapters so they could get a feel for its narrative style. Now that I was ready to sign the contract, it was time to iron out a few production details.

"I'd like to make this new book your November release," Jodi, my editor, told me. "That way we can follow up *Tidewater* with a new novel under our imprint, six months after Tidewater's re-launch."

(*Tidewater*, which I'd self-published in July of 2014, had been picked up by Lake Union in the fall, and was slated for a re-release under LU's imprint in May.)

"November sounds great to me," I said.

Jodi asked hesitantly, "How soon do you think you can get this book written? If we want to release it in November, we might need to get it through developmental edits as soon as the last week of March. I'll have to check the editors' schedules, but it could be a tight squeeze."

"No problem," I said, without a stitch of worry. "I can definitely do that."

"Uhhh," Jodi replied, "we'll need time to give it a thorough edit."

"I know," I said. "How does February 7th sound? That should give us a little more than six weeks for developmental edits."

"Are you sure you can do that?" Jodi asked. "February 7th is only three weeks away."

"Yep," I assured her. "I've done it before—written a novel of the same size in just three weeks. In fact, I've done it a couple of times. *I've already got the entire book outlined.* The story is ready to go; all it needs now is words. I can give it plenty of words in three weeks, believe me. I'll have the first draft to you by February 7th."

That same afternoon, I dusted off the outline of my new historical novel and looked back over it to re-acquaint myself with the story. I hadn't touched that outline for some time, and I'd forgotten a lot of the details of my story. But as I read the outline, I smiled, and felt confident about the book's future.

And it was little wonder that Lake Union had been so enthusiastic about the proposal. It was easy to tell just from the outline that the story was sound and whole, with a fascinating central character and a compelling plot—the kind you can't look away from. Even in outline form, the story felt *complete*, with a clear set of problems for the main character to tackle, rising tension, logical flow from one scene to the next, and an ending that felt deeply satisfying, even if it was a little bit sad. This would definitely turn out to be a good book, well-paced and rich-feeling. I had no reason to doubt it; I could assess the book's qualities in its bare bones—in its outline.

I knew my average typing speed, and even factoring in my usual two days off per week and a few extra no-work days in case of illness or emergencies, I was 100% confident that I could turn in a quality first draft by my three-week deadline. As it happened, the world's worst cold nearly did thwart my efforts, but I still managed to hand in the rough draft, all 92,000 words of it, by 10 p.m. on February 7th.

Maybe you're asking yourself how the heck any author can be so confident in her own writing that she can commit to delivering a brand-new novel in just three weeks. Maybe you've tried outlining before and can't fathom how a simple outline could give me the assurance I needed to set such a tight deadline. Maybe you think I'm totally deluded, and that I ought to rely much more on beta readers and extensive peer feedback before I decide that I can produce good books at a rapid clip.

But there really isn't any secret to gaining this kind of confidence in your work—nor is delusion necessary. When you plan a story the right way, you guarantee a tight, compelling structure that keeps readers turning pages and delivers a satisfying reading experience from start to finish. And really, a satisfied reader is all you need for a "good" book. Some might argue (with good reason) that satisfied readers are the *only* markers of quality that really matter.

 If there's any secret involved here, it's this: no matter what your genre, no matter what age group you write for, whether you write drabbles or flash fiction or short stories or epic tomes stretching over several thousand-page volumes, you *can* know *exactly* how to reach your reader—how to touch them in a way they can't ignore, how to compel them to keep turning your pages until they finally reach the end of your book... and you *can* know that your book will be good before you write it. Once you know what elements readers universally connect with, you can objectively evaluate your own books and determine for yourself whether they are "good" or not—whether their plots are sound, their characters intriguing, and their payoffs satisfying.

You see, every reader responds favorably to the same basic, deep-down, core elements of story. *Story itself* is a particular thing—a very specific *something* that we recognize by instinct. Story follows familiar patterns, and speaks to the human consciousness (and subconscious) in unique yet instantly recognizable ways.

In this short book, I'll show you how to plan out a good story before you even begin writing it, so that you can maximize your efficiency, increase your confidence in your own work, and be assured of delivering a quality product to your readers without wasting any time or embroiling yourself in anxiety over the particulars of your plot.

My method for assembling a quick-writing story is easy to follow and universal. It works equally well no matter what you write: kids' books, adult novels, memoir, and narrative nonfiction of any length.

Best of all—and most importantly—this method will dramatically increase your speed and ratchet up your production. With a little practice, it might even allow you to write a new novel in three weeks' time!

But let's be clear about what this book *is*, and what it *is not*.

Take Off Your Pants! Is a guide to help you increase your speed and efficiency as an author. It will provide you with a method for planning out a book's particulars before you begin to write—and a method for ensuring that your book will be cohesive, compelling, and satisfying.

Is the method I present in this book the only way to plot out a book? Is the type of plot structure I use with my outlines the only form a story can take? Of course not! Not at all. There are plenty of examples of great works of fiction that don't follow the same patterns I recommend in *Take Off Your Pants!* For example, James Bond doesn't go through the same character progression I recommend in this outlining method. Not all romances follow the same protagonist/antagonist patterns (a good many of them do... just in very subtle ways!) Books like *The Martian* by Andy Weir don't utilize a personal antagonist; the environment of Mars is the antagonist, and so the antagonist doesn't follow the same behavioral patterns I recommend in *Take Off Your Pants!*

My goal in writing this book wasn't to dictate the one true story structure, or to decree that all works of fiction share these same qualities. My goal was specifically to share **an** organizational method that has dramatically increased my speed and efficiency as a writer, and has allowed me to produce more books that readers love faster than I ever could before.

The method I'll teach you in this book is *one* way to approach story out of *many* possible ways. Its key benefit is the fact that it allows you to analyze a book's commercial appeal before you begin to write, thus saving you time and helping you build your writing business with speed and efficiency.

You're reading the Revised Edition of *Take Off Your Pants!* Since I first published this short book in March of 2015, I've received a truly overwhelming number of emails from writers who've found the method to be useful and inspiring. I'm so happy that my humble little outlining book has helped so many authors reach their production goals, and has helped them gain more confidence in their work. But I want to be sure that you, Reader, understand that my advice applies to improving production speed, ensuring efficiency, and giving you confidence in your ability to write "a good book." It's not intended to be the last word on story, and shouldn't be taken as such.

Now that you know what to expect from this book, are you ready to jump in? Good! But before I can show you how and why my outlining method works, we need to put paid to a very familiar debate...

Plotters > Pantsers... at least when it comes to speed

Are you a plotter or a pantser?

If you've spent any time on writers' forums, listened to writing podcasts, or read blogs about writing, you've certainly encountered this question. You've witnessed the discussion—or more likely, the debate—that the plotter/pantser query inevitably spawns.

There's no doubt that writers love to hash out the relative superiority of *plotting* (outlining the specifics of a story's action before you begin writing the story itself) versus *pantsing* (flying by the seat of your pants; going with the flow) endlessly, and in great detail, whenever the opportunity arises.

Maybe you've even asked yourself this question in your moments of quiet introspection. "Am I a plotter or a pantser? If I prefer one camp, should I force myself to switch to the other? Is one method truly superior—will one method deliver results that bring me closer to my personal goals as an author?"

Invariably, the debate over plotting versus pantsing ends in a draw—somebody, usually a forum moderator, will state that whatever method works for the individual is just fine and dandy, the thread will be locked, and riled writers will move on with their lives. (At least until the following week, when some forum newcomer will start the debate all over again.) Conventional wisdom, then, dictates that whatever method works for you simply works for you, and one is not inherently superior to the other.

In broad, general terms, I absolutely agree. If you're comfortable with your method and it delivers results you like, then it works for you, and you shouldn't fix what isn't broken.

But you're reading this book for a reason: because you want to learn how to outline in a way that increases your speed as well as your confidence in your own books. And that means you're probably not very satisfied with the method you're currently using, whether it's pantsing or plotting.

So at the risk of making myself very unpopular, I'm going to go out on a limb and state boldly that there is, in fact, a superior method for writing a book...IF—and that's a very particular "if"—your goals include establishing a full-time writing career.

Not every writer *wants* to do it full-time. Many are content to keep their writing relegated to the realm of the hobby—something they do to unwind, to explore their creativity, and to feel accomplished. There is absolutely nothing wrong with hobby-writing. Some magnificent works have been produced by authors who were not full-timers, and who never aspired to be full-timers. If you're an author who is perfectly happy to write for fun, then pantsing may work just as well for you as plotting—or it may work better! In the case of the contented hobby writer, there is not a superior method for approaching the writing process.

If, however, you want to write for a living— whether you plan to self-publish all your titles or take the split traditional/indie "hybrid" route— *speed and volume will be critical to achieving your professional goals.*

(If your goal is to traditionally publish *only*, without an indie component to your business, it's my opinion that you shouldn't plan to ever quit your day job. It's exceedingly rare nowadays, and getting rarer all the time, for a traditional-only author to make enough money to support himself or herself. If you have a family, or would like to have one someday, your chances of being able to afford to give up the day job are even smaller. Fortunately for all of us, now we have the option to self-publish or to combine the two career tracks, as I've done—and that makes for a much more attainable career goal!)

I get that my opinion on this topic isn't popular with some authors—both my parenthetical above, and the statement that came before it. I've seen the ticked-off reviews of this book, and the discussions on writing forums that talk about how *wrong* I am to claim that speed is essential to a writing career. I understand that it's not necessarily what some folks want to hear. But it *is* true—take it from somebody who writes fiction full-time!—and it's becoming truer every day.

There was an era when authors could make a living by writing only one or two books a year. There are still a few authors who manage to do just that. (Most of them have been established in the publishing business for a long time, and are holdovers from those prior days.) But as technology advances and eager indies bring more books to market with greater speed, even the long-established traditionally published authors struggle to keep up.

Reader demand for more books is growing apace with indie production. *Speed* (relative to what popular authors in your genre manage to produce) has become a major factor in authorial success. Why the heck do you think Nora Roberts/J.D. Robb writes so many books a year? She has enough dough to retire in the Bahamas if she wants to, I'm sure. But she continues to produce good books at a fast clip because that's how an author keeps his or her brand relevant in today's fast-paced, high-demand publishing environment.

Full-time authors in *all* sectors of publishing—indie, traditional, or hybrid, and in every genre—agree that the more books you have for sale, the easier it is to make money. The higher your volume—the greater your quantity of available titles—the more opportunities you have to reach new readers and to direct them from one book to the next, and the next, and the next. More books naturally mean more sales.

In order to build up a substantial volume of titles before you're in your grave, you must be able to write quickly enough that you can turn out several books per year. It *is* do-able, as my three-week-deadline anecdote showed—but that kind of speed requires the meticulous organization and the *confidence* in the quality of your story that can only come from outlining before you begin.

There certainly are authors who can manage speed and volume while still flying by the seat of their pants! I admire them greatly, and I'm even a little jealous of their mystical ability, because I *love* abandoning my outlines and just writing off into the wild blue yonder. It's fun! It's creatively stimulating! It's an amazing adventure, which I try to take as often as my schedule permits. If I could consistently write un-outlined books fast enough to support my career, I'd wear party hats all day long and do a happy-dance every time I stood up from my writing chair.

But I'm just not one of those authors. And since you're reading this book, it's a pretty safe bet that you aren't one of those lucky ducks, either. You're reading this book because you're looking for a method that will help you achieve your goals in a realistic timeframe.

If you're already very fond of pantsing, I don't want you to think I'm trashing the process. Just because I think that outlining is a sounder *business strategy* for the majority of full-time (or aspiring full-time) authors doesn't mean I don't appreciate all the perks of pantsing. I know darn well that some absolutely glorious books have been written via the "pantsing" method. I also know the particular joy of discovery that flying by the seat of your pants can bring. The act of writing without a pre-arranged structure has an awful lot to recommend for it. It's creatively stimulating, and allows for experimentation and freedom that you won't typically get by following a pre-planned outline (though, as you'll see, my outlining method does allow for lots of creative "wiggle room.") For writers who just want to explore their landscapes—language, character, their own minds—pantsing is fantastic, and can produce spectacular works.

But if your goals include quitting your day job

and staying out of an office cubicle for the next several years—and if you're not one of those rare birds who can fly very fast by the seat of his pants and still produce high-quality books— then effective outlining is a skill you *must* learn. Without it, you will never have the assurance that you *can* produce several books per year, that you *can* stick to a regular production schedule, that your backlist *will* grow at a rate that will support your business—or that you *can* meet a very tight deadline for your publisher.

Allow me to illustrate my point with two examples from my own list of titles.

Baptism for the Dead is a pretty little work of literary fiction that I published in 2012. Reviews from readers have consistently been very positive. It's a gorgeous novel, if I do say so myself, sure to please fans of the literary genre. At just over 60,000 words, it took me **two freaking years** to complete, because I had no specific plan before I set out to write it. No outline, no knowledge of where it was going—it was as pantsy as pantsing can possibly get. It's lovely, very fulfilling for me on a personal level, and one of the best things I've ever written. I'm terribly glad that I wrote it, even though, like most literary novels, it doesn't sell a staggering number of copies per year.

But in spite of my love for that book, the business-woman in me shudders to think of all the time I spent chipping away slowly at *Baptism* when I could have written *at least* a dozen other novels during those two years.

And I'm not kidding about that number. Even that early in my career, I could have easily written a dozen more books in the time I spent pantsing around with *Baptism for the Dead* if I'd only been outlining—and outlining the right way.

Just after the New Year in 2013, I spent a day outlining a new novel, *The Crook and Flail*. The next day I began writing. Twenty-one days later, I had completed the first draft of this 90,000-word historical novel. In three weeks, I produced a book that was half again as long as *Baptism for the Dead* thanks to a useful outline.

And I can tell you that *The Crook and Flail* sells far more copies than *Baptism*. *Crook* is, in fact, still one of the mainstays of my business, more than a year and a half after it was published.

I hope these examples from my own career illustrate why I so firmly believe that any author who has professional aspirations must learn the skill of effective outlining.

If you love the vast creative flexibility of pantsing, take heart: you don't have to outline all the time. As much as I believe in the power of my outlining method, even I don't apply it to every book I write. Sometimes I still enjoy the flexibility and discovery of writing without any sort of guide.

In fact, I'm working on another literary novel now (in my spare time, since I expect it to follow in *Baptism*'s footsteps and earn me... not a lot of money) and with that project, I'm flying by the seat of my pants all the way.

But for my commercial books—the ones I depend on to earn my living; the ones I schedule for regular releases and intend to strike a chord with a wide audience—it's outlining or nothing.

So you see, when it comes to the eternal quandary of pantsing or plotting, you can keep a foot in each camp. But if your goals will require you to write with speed and confidence, an effective outline will be your best friend. Once you know the skill, it will be just another tool in your kit, ready to pull out when it's just the right gadget for the task at hand.

What do you say? Do you want to learn how to use this powerful tool? Do you want to put effective, solid outlining to work for you, so that you can improve your speed, increase efficiency, and grow confidence in your own writing? Are you willing to plunge into the outlining process?

Great! Then it's time to let go of your old pantsing ways. Take off your pants, and follow me!

The Core of Every Story

Before I begin teaching you the specifics of my outlining method—before you can run freely through the literary wilds, sans pants—let's talk about *why* this method works so well, and why you can apply it to your writing regardless of the age of your audience, your genre, or the length of the work.

Remember earlier in this book, when I said that *story* is a very particular thing—and that every reader responds favorably to certain deep-down, core elements of story? It's absolutely true—and it's such a ubiquitous feature of narrative writing (and of the reading experience) that you probably aren't even aware of it. Most people aren't, even if they've been reading and writing for decades. When I finally figured this out, I walked around starry-eyed for days, struck by this colossal "A-ha!!!" moment.

The ability to identify a story's true heart—and to see that it is *exactly the same as the heart of every other good story*, when you really get down to the brass tacks—is a real revelation. It's also, paradoxically, a total "No duh!" moment. In the same instant that you grasp what *story* really is, and gain that magical ability to identify the true core of *any* story, you also realize that it was staring you in the face all along. You just didn't notice it because sound story structure is so familiar to all of us that we don't see it unless we know we ought to look for it.

The outlining method I'll teach you has this Story Core at its heart. Yes, I'm going to capitalize that phrase from here on out, because it's very important, and I want you to remember it. Everything else you learn in this book will build on the Story Core, so take a few moments to ponder the Core and then apply it to all the good stories you've ever consumed—via reading, watching movies or TV, watching a ballet or opera, etc.

The Story Core

Every compelling story has the following five elements:

1. A character

2. The character wants something

3. But something prevents him from getting what he wants easily

4. So he struggles against that force

5. And either succeeds or fails

The Story Core is *always* there, in every good book. Sometimes its elements can be a little misty and vague and difficult to discern. But if the story compels, you'll find the Story Core at its heart. It doesn't matter whether it's an action-packed sci-fi adventure or a romance or a kids' picture book or an introspective literary novel that appears to focus more on pretty prose than on a definable plot. If you feel compelled to keep reading, you'll find the Story Core at work.

And when the Story Core is treated with the outlining method I'll teach you in the pages ahead, it grabs hold of the human mind and makes it virtually impossible for a reader to look away.

Don't believe me that the Story Core is at the center of every good book? Let's look at a few examples, ranging across several different genres. We'll revisit a few of these examples later in the book (and look at some new examples, too) to illustrate how the Story Core concept can be effectively expanded through the steps of a complete outline.

Charlotte's Web by **E.B. White** Wilbur the pig wants a lot of things over the course of his story, but maybe his most pressing desire is to stay alive! He's afraid that once the county fair is over, he'll be killed and served up as bacon unless he can make himself seem like much more than an ordinary pig. So with the help of his resourceful friends, he concocts a sort of "publicity campaign" to make himself seem miraculous. In the end, his life is saved.

Lolita by **Vladimir Nabokov** Humbert Humbert is a man with a deplorable attraction to young girls. He wants to possess not only the body, but also the heart and mind of Lolita, the object of his obsession. He wants her to love him as he "loves" her. So, acting out of selfishness, he effectively kidnaps her and remains constantly on the move, isolating her from peers and adults who might help her, in an attempt to create the kind of realtionship he wants. But in the end, Lolita finally manages to give him the slip and constructs a normal life beyond his influence—and ultimately dies, leaving Humbert forever unable to reach his goal.

The Cat in the Hat by **Dr. Seuss** Bored on a rainy day, two children initially just want to have a little fun. But then the Cat in the Hat appears, bringing entirely too much fun—the kind that will get them in serious trouble if their mother finds out! When the Cat refuses to rein in the good times, Things 1 and 2 must be captured before Mom comes home.

The cat, finally seeing the error of his ways, helps clean up the house just in time to avoid landing the kids in serious trouble.

***To Kill a Mockingbird* by Harper Lee** Like many complex novels that deal with difficult or weighty themes, Scout and the other characters in *To Kill a Mockingbird* want a lot of different things throughout the course of the book. But what Scout wants most—the *external goal* for her portion of the story (we'll talk about that concept later on)—is knowledge about Boo Radley. This mysterious character fascinates her, and her desire to figure out who he is and what made him so strange and reclusive is one of many reflections on the novel's theme: combatting prejudice. After many attempts to catch sight of Boo (most of them ill-advised), Scout comes face to face with Boo when he saves her and her brother from an attacker. She is finally able to see Boo not as a legend or a monster, but as a real human being who has feelings and needs not unlike her own.

***The Wonderful Wizard of Oz* by L. Frank Baum** When Dorothy finds herself swept off to a magical but foreign land, all she wants is to return home to Kansas. But she is recruited into the political machinations of Oz, and manipulated by the Wizard into performing an assassination. After many dangerous adventures, one mishap after another thwarts Dorothy's attempts to get home. But at last, when she and her friends have overcome their various personal weaknesses, she learns that the power to achieve her goal was always with her, and she returns safely to Kansas.

In these examples—five stories that appear very different on the surface—you can see the exact same Story Core at work. You can observe for yourself how the same bare-bones, deep-rooted elements are always at the heart of every good story. That Story Core provides the hook that snags a reader's attention and pulls them into the world you've created. Without a complete Story Core— without all five parts working in harmony—you can't construct a solid outline, and you can't write a compelling book.

The Three-Legged Outline

Of course, not all outlines are created equal.

Lots of authors have given outlining a shot. Many of them have found it to be too restrictive, so that they felt compelled to stick to exactly the plan they'd laid out, even when they got into the meat of the story and felt that events were really pulling their plot in a different direction. Other authors have found it to be a pointless waste of time, since figuring out what happens in advance didn't really assist them in any meaningful way when it came to actually writing the story. Still others found that it sapped their enthusiasm for the book—once they knew all the particulars of the plot, they lost interest in actually writing it.

Maybe your past experiences with outlining have been similar. But those of you who tried to outline a book and didn't see much benefit from it simply didn't do it the right way. Sorry to be the bearer of bad news.

But take heart! There is absolutely a *right* way to outline a book—one that allows you plenty of creative freedom in the particulars of your plot, gives you a well-drawn map to guide your story through an arc you know will be compelling, and can still leave much of the plot a total mystery to you, if that's the way you prefer to write.

The right kind of outline follows a particular structure, with a three-sided form—and so the structure is the first thing you'll need to learn.

Of course, that doesn't mean your *book* has to follow a rigid or "formulaic" structure. You can apply this outline structure to all kinds of experimental writing—moving forward and backward in time, for example.

As you read on and expand your understanding of the outlining process, you'll see the "shape" of this outline branch out and develop all kinds of offshoots. However, you can visualize your outline in its most basic form as the Story Core (the five steps we explored in the previous section) sitting on top of a three-legged stool.

This three-legged stool supports the Core of your story. As with a real-life stool, if one of your legs is missing, the whole structure will topple, and your Story Core will roll off across the floor, collecting dust bunnies and goobers as it goes, and looking pretty unappealing as a result.

Each of your three legs is equally important, too. If one is shorter than the others—that is, if you don't put as much care into developing one "leg" as you put into the other two—your story will feel rickety and precarious, and just won't sit comfortably with the reader.

But build all three legs sturdily, with equal attention, and you've got a secure, elegant base on which to rest your Story Core.

The Three-Legged Outline consists of:

*Character Arc

*Theme

*Pacing

I'll break down each "leg" in the chapters to come. But first, note what's missing from this structure: *Plot*.

Plot is defined as "the main events of a...novel... or similar work, devised and presented by the writer as an interlaced sequence." Plot is your sequence of events—the order in which things happen; their interlacing; the "action" that goes on outside of a character, beyond the range of his inner experience, but certainly influencing his inner experience.

31

There's a reason why it's missing from the Three-Legged Outline. Many writers picture (or practice) outlining as stringing together a *plot*—setting up events in a logical sequence and interlacing them so that there is a feeling of cause and effect. That's an important part of outlining, but it should actually be your *very last* step, and it's entirely mutable.

Plot's mutability—its lack of grounding in the Story Core—makes some plot-centric outlines frustrating to work with. An outline that is just a plot, with one event following another and little consideration given to other facets of the story, might lead you into several dead-ends, throw unexpected road blocks in your path, and leave you with an unsatisfying final product. Ultimately, it will probably waste more time than you'd hoped, and will give you no benefit over taking the "pants" approach.

Remember that *plot* is not the same thing as *story*—at least, not within the context of this book, or within the practice of outlining.

Plot is certainly a *part* of constructing a story. It's a *factor* in outlining. But believe it or not, it's the least important factor. If you focus your efforts on the Three Legs—character arc, pacing, and theme—you can change the specifics of the plot a hundred different times, and you'll still have essentially the same story.

This is why I asserted earlier in this ebook that you can outline a novel and still give yourself considerable creative "wiggle room." If you're the kind of author who loves to discover twists and turns as you write, you can leave nearly all of the plot *out* of your outline. You can discover the plot as you go—but you'll still have a solid core for your story, which will give you assurance that your story will always be complete and compelling, even if you decide to change the plot entirely on the second draft!

In the upcoming pages, I'll take you through the process of structuring your outline, focusing on each of the three "legs" of your sturdy tripod, and showing you how to relate each leg to the Story Core. This will maximize the strength of your outline—it will provide you with objective assurance that your story is on the right track, and will deliver a reading experience that is both compelling and ultimately satisfying.

I'll also show you how to develop the events of your plot by focusing on Story Core, character arc, and theme. This, too, will ensure that your plot remains relevant and gripping.

That being said, I don't want you to be confused by the order in which I present this information. I just expended all these words telling you that all three legs of the outline are equally important, and that the specifics of your plot are the least crucial part of an effective outline. Yet we'll go through the outlining method in the following order:

1. Character Arc

2. Theme

3. Plot

4. Pacing

Why this order? Because in practical terms, it's natural and logical to develop your story in this order. But don't let the order fool you. The plot is always subject to change. It can wiggle and shift and alter itself completely if you like. As long as it relates to the three-legged support and the Story Core, your outline will still be just as effective. But without equal attention paid to the character arc, theme, and pacing, any other component of your outline might fall apart, and the cohesion and quality of your story might be in danger.

In other words, don't let pacing slide just because it's last on the list. It's the key to delivering the kind of page-turning experience that keeps readers coming back for more!

Character Arc: Start With a Flaw

All right, so if *plot*—a sequence of events—isn't the same thing as story, then what *is* story?

Simply put, a story is a character arc—a personality making a progression from an emotional or psychological Point A to an emotional or psychological Point B. Story is all about internal growth, not external events. It's a character's struggle to shed old behaviors or beliefs that have held him back from becoming his "true self"—the person he was always "meant to be."

It sounds a little hokey at first blush, I know—but this "struggle to grow into the Meant To Be" has been with humanity for as long as we've had writing—and doubtless was part of our culture, our learning, and our entertainment long before humans first developed writing. The struggle to grow, to learn how to be a better person, is a theme that is constantly repeated in mythology across the world. This surely indicates that it plucks at a very deep and important chord in the human psyche. When you follow the example of ancient myth, you're tapping into an idea that every reader can connect to on a subconscious—even instinctive—level.

That's why character arc, *not* plot, is at the center of my outlining method. Without a complete character arc underpinning it, *any* plot will feel totally irrelevant. I don't care how many explosions it has, how many rampaging dinosaurs, how evil your villain is, or how twisty your twist is—if I don't feel invested in your central character, the plot just won't excite me.

But if I am interested in your character, then even the quietest, simplest plot will feel compelling and important.

(Even characters who don't appear to make complete character arcs, such as James Bond, still touch on *elements* of character progression. Think how many times Bond gets into trouble by chasing after a hot spy-lady. If only he could shed his womanizing ways, his life and his missions would be so much easier! That *need to change* influences his many stories, although we're always left with the same, reliable old Bond by the end of each installment.)

Many writers—especially young writers or other raw beginners—feel that the way to make a reader care about a character is to give them special traits that nobody else has. Extreme beauty, awesome magical powers, a super-quick mind that can solve any crime... these can all be fascinating parts of a plot, but by themselves, they don't bear much on character.

The earliest advice many new writers receive when they seek out their first critiques is some variation on "Make your character sympathetic." Usually this advice is administered in response to one of these ultra-awesome but personality-lacking characters.

However, virtually nobody knows what "Make your character sympathetic" actually *means*. I sure as heck don't know. What *does* it mean? Is a "sympathetic" character an orphan, all alone in the cruel world? Has a "sympathetic" character been denied some great opportunity? Does a "sympathetic" character have some endearing flaw, like clumsiness or shyness?

"Make your character sympathetic" is perhaps the most common advice I see handed out to new writers. Alas, it's almost never offered up with supplemental advice on *how* one goes about accomplishing it. It's left up to the new author to figure out, and so the remedy they choose is often to attach a "flaw" or a social handicap (such as being orphaned) to their otherwise-awesome MC.

Even many experienced authors with several books

under their belts still fall into this trap. They "make their character sympathetic" by picking a few "flaw" traits from a laundry list, and they figure that's good enough to give the reader some sort of investment in the character. It's typically not enough, and it will lead to books being abandoned as often as they're finished.

Recall that *character arc* is one of the three legs that make up the foundation of your outline—of your book. A character arc is a progression from an emotional Point A to an emotional Point B. The word *progression* implies that Point B is an improvement over Point A, doesn't it? Therefore, the way to create an arc—the way to invest a reader in your book—is to start with a character that needs some improvement.

In other words, don't make your character *sympathetic*. Make your character *flawed*. And I'm not talking about endearing, cutesy flaws, like clumsiness or shyness or unusually colored eyes, that don't have any stakes attached to them. Make your character flawed in a serious, big, scary, potentially life-wrecking way. When you start with a badly flawed character, the arc will be all about correcting that flaw—about your character growing into a better person, the kind of mythic hero archetype he was "meant to be" but couldn't become until this adventure—the events of your plot—pushed him to change himself for the better.

We all love an attempt to change for the better, even if that attempt ultimately fails (and it is perfectly okay to make your character fail at the end of his arc—and fail spectacularly! Think how Ned Stark ended up in *A Game of Thrones*.) We love to root for a person who's trying to make the epic hero's journey (read Joseph Campbell's book *The Hero with a Thousand Faces* if you don't know what I'm talking about.) We've loved to root for that struggling, changing, self-bettering hero since time immemorial. The self-bettering hero speaks to our deepest instincts and makes for a story that we just can't stop reading.

I first came to really understand the importance of starting a book with a character's serious flaw when I read *The Anatomy of Story: 22 Steps to Becoming a Master Storyteller*, by John Truby. Truby's book provides a fantastic look at story construction from start to finish, with lots of useful examples, but it's geared mostly toward screenwriters who are making stories for a film-viewing audience. While many aspects of story are the same whether you're talking about film or books, not all of them are. So to give credit where it's due, I've built much of my own outlining/story construction methods using John Truby's 22-step method as a guide. But I've streamlined much of his process to suit the particulars of writing for a *reading* audience, and added plenty of my own observations and experiences, as well.

However, Truby's assertion that all compelling stories start with the main character's big internal flaw is spot on, whether you're talking about books or movies. When the audience understands that the main character has a very serious need to change his own heart and mind, the hook is set, and the audience is irrevocably invested.

(Incidentally, a few readers have contacted me to tell me that they'd like more examples of the points I make in *Take Off Your Pants!* I'm the type of person who feels that one example of each point is enough, so I haven't added any additional illustrations of my points to this revised edition. However, if you would like a wealth of detailed examples of various components of story structure, I can heartily recommend Truby's book. He provides multiple examples for each of the bullet points in his lessons.)

Character Arc: Make the Flaw Serious

Let's talk for a while longer about your main character's flaw. It's crucial to your story, because it serves two very important purposes.

First, the flaw sets a hook in the reader, giving them a reason to truly care about your character—and therefore, about your book. The presence of a flaw signals to the reader that this is a character who has the potential to become a true hero by the book's end. The presence of a hero triggers our instinctive attraction to story—the promise of a hero's journey signals to the reader's subconscious mind that this will be a meaty, juicy story, likely to deliver a satisfying payoff for all the time spent reading it.

Second, the character's flaw will narrow down your story choices considerably. Once you decide on a flaw, the external events you choose—the plot—must provide a logical framework for your character's arc. They must provide stepping stones

41

for him to eventually, after trial and error, make it from Point A to Point B, and to end up as a person who has changed for the better (or failed in the attempt.) Your character's flaw will dictate the inciting event, the antagonist, the ally, and the "false starts" he makes at bettering himself.

In order for a flaw to feel compelling, it has to provide an obvious obstacle to your character's growth. It has to hold him back in some meaningful way, keeping him trapped in an uncomfortable state.

Perhaps, for example, your character finds it difficult to trust members of the opposite sex. Or perhaps she has a secret terror of dogs that keeps her shut inside her home all day, for fear that she'll be attacked by a chihuahua. Maybe your character needs to learn to trust her own judgment, or to stop being so pompous, or to be kinder to the people she loves.

Whatever flaw you choose, it must be serious—it has to prevent your character from living life to its fullest, or from achieving full actualization of self—or it can even cause your character to hurt other people. As long as the flaw is causing measurable harm to your character's life or to the lives of those around her, it's fair game.

You certainly don't have to use any of the options I provided above in your story (though you can if you'd like to!) And just because you're starting each book by thinking up *a* character flaw, that doesn't mean your books will feel formulaic or all the same. Think about all the inner difficulties real people face. You've got a virtually endless buffet of psychological dysfunction from which to choose!

I've used a wide variety of character flaws to great effect in my own books, and because the main characters' flaws are so different, none of the books feel like the same-old, same-old, even to readers who have gone through my entire catalog. Here's an illustration of the many ways one author can put a character's flaw at the center of her books, and still write a lot of very different books: Ahmose in *The Sekhmet Bed* is naïve, and believes that she can do no wrong as long as she thinks she has the gods' blessing. The nameless narrator in *Baptism for the Dead* has allowed herself to stay in a stifling situation for too long. In *Tidewater*, Pocahontas craves a high status she was not born into, and will do just about anything to get it; John Smith is bitter and thinks little of other people; and Opechancanough is too quick to solve his problems with violence. Daughter of Sand and Stone, that book I wrote under the three-week deadline, has a main character who just can't seem to rid herself of dangerous levels of hubris.

Don't fear that your books will feel "all the same" if you put a character's inner troubles front and center. Trust me on this one: they'll feel *plenty* different enough to keep your readers thrilled.

But do remember that whatever flaw you choose for your main character, it must be a big one—it has to have far greater consequences than having a gap in her teeth or being a clutz.

The flaw must also be something the character is capable of changing—something she can conceivably grow out of, if she makes the right decisions along her journey. For example, if you have a character who's paralyzed from the waist down, his paralysis can't be his character flaw. He can't grow out of that. But dwelling on his situation, refusing to accept his limitations, and refusing to see his many strengths that have nothing to do with use of his legs. Any or *all* of those traits can certainly count as character flaws.

Let's look at some more examples. I'll lay out a few stories that should be familiar to you, point out the character's flaw at the beginning of the book, his "hero status" at the end (after he's overcome his flaw and changed for the better), and list a few ways the hero's flaw has dictated other key aspects of the story. You'll see how the authors of these books have used various components of story to reflect, amplify, and mold the character's flaw, pushing him toward his hero status as an improved person.

Charlotte's Web by E.B. White

Main character: Wilbur, a pig.

Flaw: Wilbur's twin fears of death and loss prevent him from enjoying life.

Hero status: By the end of the book, Wilbur has learned that death is inevitable, but that even in the midst of grief, the cycle of life offers us renewed joy and hope. He has made peace with his fears and is seen as a more sensible, stable "person" than he was at the beginning of the story.

How the flaw shaped the book: Since one of Wilbur's greatest fears is death, he must be confronted by its specter again and again until he finally overcomes his flaw. First, he is nearly killed because he's the runt of the litter. Later, he begins a campaign, along with his barnyard friends, to establish himself as a celebrity, so that Farmer Zuckerman won't kill him for his meat. But in the climax of the book, he learns that even as a celebrity, he cannot escape death—he must confront the loss of his dearest friend, Charlotte the spider, before he can conquer his flaw and achieve his hero status. If Wilbur's flaw hadn't involved a fear of death, there would be no point in weaving this theme of confronting death and grief into the plot.

Lolita by Vladimir Nabokov

Main character: Humbert Humbert

Flaw: Humbert is entirely self-centered, always putting his own lust ahead of other people's needs.

Hero status: By losing everything he once enjoyed, including control of Lolita, his health, and even his freedom, Humbert comes to understand how much of a despicable person he's been all along. *Lolita* is a great example of how a main character can fail to achieve his plot-based goals, but can still deliver a satisfying reading experience by overcoming his personal flaws and progressing to a higher state of self-awareness.

How the flaw shaped the book: Humbert is so selfish that you can't even trust his narration—most of the time, anyway. He leads you to believe that Lolita was not his victim, that she was complicit in and even welcoming of her abuse. But now and then, a stray snippet or fleeting image will slide through Humbert's slick words, showing the reader how Lolita really felt. As the book continues toward its climax, where Humbert meets Lolita again when she is married and pregnant, mistress of her own home, smoking a cigarette, and in control of an adult life and an adult identity, Humbert's bombast collapses, and he sees himself for the monster he truly is. He knows he cannot undo the damage he's done to Lolita, but the fact that he has finally relinquished his selfish behavior and truly regrets the pain he's caused provides a satisfying ending. Nabokov used the "unreliable narrator" motif to illustrate Humbert's flaw, and then dramatically shattered that carefully built façade to expose Humbert's terrible flaw to the character himself, in one dramatic scene.

Harry Potter and the Sorcerer's Stone by J.K. Rowling

(Or *Harry Potter and the Philosopher's Stone*, for those of you who aren't North American.)

Main character: Harry Potter, a boy wizard.

Flaw: Harry is meek and unsure of himself, and hasn't yet embraced his destiny as a powerful hero.

Hero status: Although Harry gets close to achieving his hero status by the end of this book, he's not quite there yet. However, he has overcome much of the meekness and self-doubt that plagued him at the beginning, and the reader gets a clear sense that with more experience (and gripping adventures), Harry will finally become the hero he is meant to be.

How the flaw shaped the book: Harry's story is about as classic-myth as it gets—and that's what gives the *Harry Potter* series such spectacular appeal across a very broad audience. Harry's flaw is the same flaw that many mythic heroes had in the best-loved stories of ages gone by: he must grow from boy to man—that is, he must grow from meek and uncertain to a strong leader, capable of making good decisions and protecting those he loves.

This flaw is reflected and explored many times throughout the book (and in subsequent volumes in the series—and don't worry, I'll discuss plotting character arcs across an entire series later in this book.) At first, Harry lives with his abusive aunt and uncle, so afraid to assert himself that he sleeps in a cupboard under the stairs. When he decides to go to Hogwarts against his relatives' wishes, he takes the first step toward overcoming his flaw— but it's not as easy as that. His meekness still haunts him, and shows itself in many ways, from his fear about the Sorting Hat to his confrontations with Snape and Draco.

When he and Ron defy the teachers' orders and venture out to save Hermione from the troll, he takes another step toward his goal, but he's not there yet. In the climax of the book, when Harry comes face to face with Voldemort, his internal goal finally seems to be within his grasp—but it slips away from him. Harry is not able to conquer his antagonist; Dumbledore must rescue him, and the audience understands that although Harry has learned much about leadership and bravery, he's not yet ready to claim full hero status. This is a perfect setup for a long-running series, which will carry on with more of Harry's attempts to overcome his flaw.

However, if Harry's flaw weren't meekness and lack of confidence, it would make little sense to put him through so many trials that test the limits of his bravery and require him to step into the role of a leader.

If, for example, Harry's flaw was that he was selfish and vain, like Humbert Humbert in *Lolita*, then repeated trials of bravery and leadership would feel irrelevant. If his flaw was fear of death, like Wilbur in *Charlotte's Web*, trials of leadership would also feel pointless. The plot would seem unrelated to the character, and the events of the story would feel disjointed, confusing, and strange.

I hope these examples have helped you understand how important your main character's flaw is—not only to the character arc, but to the specifics of the plot, too. The character's flaw will shape every other aspect of your book. The flaw is the engine that drives your entire book, from hooking your reader's interest to propelling the plot to its climax—so choose your flaw with care, and make it count.

The Pants Come Off
(Beginning Your Outline)

Once you know your main character's flaw, the rest of your outline will start to come together with surprising ease. Recall that a story is a character's journey from an emotional Point A to an emotional Point B—a quest to overcome his flaw. With your flaw firmly in mind, get out a piece of paper (several, actually) or better yet, pull up a fresh, blank file on your computer and prepare to save what you'll write down for future use on many future books.

It's time to truly take off your pants, and begin outline!

I'll use the outline for one of my three main characters from *Tidewater* to show you how to fill in the various parts of an outline, and how to bounce aspects of the outline off each other to develop the specifics of your story. I am using

Tidewater as an example not because I think it's the greatest book ever written (though it is pretty good!) but simply because *I outlined it*. I know what the outlining process looked like for this story; I can comment intelligently on how I chose various features of this story, how I related them to one another, and how those choices strengthened the story and eased the writing process.

Not having written *Lolita* or *Harry Potter and the Sorcerer's Stone* (too bad for me on both counts), nor any other book by any other author, I can't substitute another author's work in these outlining examples. To do so would be presumptuous and frankly rather silly.

So please take my use of *my own book* in these examples for what it is: honest communication of the way a specific outline came together, and not some sort of proclamation that my book is *like totally the greatest book ever written, you guys!*

With that disclaimer out of the way... onward!

First write down a 1. Next to it, write your character's name and any really important features we need to know about her—anything that might influence the setting. For example: *Main character: Wilbur, a pig* or *Main character: Pocahontas, a Native girl of the Powhatan tribe living in 1607.*

Beneath that line, number the next lines 2 – 5. If you guessed that you'll be filling in your Story

Core here, you guessed correctly.

Skip a line, and below your numbered lines, write *Flaw:* and then fill in the flaw you've decided upon. If you've been tinkering with the idea of a few potential flaws but haven't settled on one yet, write them all down. You can cross out or delete some later as you work through the character arc and narrow your focus.

Right now your outline should look like this:

> 1. *Main character: Pocahontas, a Native girl of the Powhatan tribe living in 1607.*
>
> 2. *[blank]*
>
> 3. *[blank]*
>
> 4. *[blank]*
>
> 5. *[blank]*
>
> *Flaw: Too driven by ambition. She steps on others in her attempts to attain glory.*

(Interjected note: You're probably intending to read this book all the way through before you begin outlining—that's smart of you—and intending to come back and work through some of all of its points once you're actually working on your own outline. With that in mind, *bookmark this page now*, and come back to this point when you're ready to actually begin writing your outline. You'll thank me for that later. You'll be able to record an entire outline in your word processor, save it, and then re-open that file later, strip out all the elements of your first outlined book, and replace them with elements of your next book. *Voila*, your own outline template!)

Now that you know your character's flaw, you can see where she needs to end up by the close of the story.

How do you determine where your character needs to end up? That's easy! Just look for the mental or emotional stance that's opposite of your character's flaw. For example, Wilbur the pig, who fears death at the beginning of his story, will need to make peace with death by the end. Pocahontas will need to learn that status isn't everything, that her ambition can be harmful to herself and others, and that helping others instead of using them is a better way to live.

If you know your character's flaw, you already know the lesson she must learn as she goes on her inner journey. Now it's only a question of whether you want to give your character a hard lesson— one in which she doesn't achieve her external goal, but learns how to be a better person—or a soft lesson—one in which she achieves her external goal, but even better, she also learns how to be a better person. You might also choose an ambiguous lesson—one that can fall into the hard or soft category, depending on how you look at it.

Humbert Humbert's lesson is hard. He ends up alone and imprisoned, doing penance for his many crimes, deprived of the love he wants. Even worse, he must live with the truth about himself—the fact he's finally been forced to confront, that he's a monster who abused Lolita and other people, too. He doesn't achieve his external goal of possessing Lolita forever, but because he regrets his actions, he does overcome his flaw. That provides a satisfying ending even though his external goal wasn't met.

Wilbur's lesson is soft. He achieves his external goal of saving his own life. True, he loses Charlotte along the way, and is forced to confront the specter of death after all. However, the fact that he gets to live with Charlotte's children (and their descendants) provides a clear comfort to temper his sorrow. He will not be lonely, and will always have a reminder of the friend he loved. He has won his external battle and his internal battle, too.

My book *Tidewater* has three main characters, each with his or her own character arc. I intentionally made each character's lesson ambiguous. I usually write ambiguous lessons for my characters;

my characters' journeys nearly always end on a note that isn't obviously positive or negative. As a reader, I'm most attracted to these types of endings. I find them intriguing and moving, and far more satisfying than black-or-white finales, so I put ambiguity into most of my books.

By the end of *Tidewater*, Pocahontas has learned to give up her ambition and has made herself a "sacrificial lamb," serving her people by trying to forge some kind of alliance with the English in order to preserve her culture. She now values her people above herself, so she has overcome her flaw. She also understands that her people won't be around much longer, so no matter what she does, she will lose the very thing for which she has made this difficult sacrifice. And yet her new life with the English is not without its happiness. She loves her husband and her son. Even knowing that she will surely lose her battle, there is much to be grateful for.

So is Pocahontas's lesson hard or soft? It's a little of both, really.

Line 5 in your Story Core is for the ending of your book. It details whether your character succeeds or fails in her *external goal*—the goal that's related to the plot, not the story—the external objective she's pursuing. You might not have any idea about her external goal yet. That's okay. You know the character's flaw; therefore, you know where she'll be by the end of the story.

On the "5" line in your Story Core, sketch out the ending in very broad terms, showing whether the character overcomes her flaw (remember, it's valid for your character to fail) and providing information about whether the lesson is hard, soft, or ambiguous.

By now, your outline should look like this:

1. Main character: Pocahontas, a Native girl of the Powhatan tribe living in 1607.

2. [blank]

3. [blank]

4. [blank]

5. End: Has given up on all ambitions. Sacrificing for her people. Ambiguous.

Flaw: Too driven by ambition. She steps on others in her attempts to attain glory.

Line 2 of your Story Core represents the character's external goal. The external goal is plot-centered; it's the outside motivation that's pushing your character along her arc. It's the carrot dangling from the stick, the thing she's trying to get—and probably for reasons which *she* thinks have nothing to do with her internal flaw. It's just *the thing she wants*, but of course *you* know that her external goal must be related to her internal flaw.

The external goal should provide an opportunity, eventually, somewhere along the path of the book, for your character to recognize her internal flaw. It should be a desire that forces her to confront her weakness, and to decide whether or not she'll embark on a journey to overcome that weakness and emerge with hero status.

Maybe your main character is a male thief, whose flaw is that he doesn't trust women. He needs to overcome that flaw by learning to view women as individuals, not as one faceless mass whom he cannot trust. Therefore, his external goal must present an opportunity for him to confront his flaw and choose whether he'll discard it for a more heroic view—one that gives all people individuality and an equal chance to prove themselves. What scenarios would present such an opportunity? Maybe a priceless diamond he'd like to steal. He knows its whereabouts, but he also knows that the only person who has the skill to retrieve it from its tricky vault is a particular cat burglar... who happens to be a woman! He's going to have to get over his mistrust and learn to work effectively with a female partner if he wants to get that diamond.

It's easy to see the dramatic potential in an action-packed goal like a jewel heist. But what about stories that call for subtler goals, or goals that are more personal to the character, and not so obviously awesome to the reader? (Who wouldn't love to have a huge, priceless diamond?!) In the case of setting deeply personal external goals for my characters, I always let the stakes be my guide.

Here's an example. If my Pocahontas must end up as a person who has given up all her old ambitions, a *big* ambition will provide much more drama, won't it? Small stakes don't offer much in the way of drama. Her change from ambitious to self-sacrificing has to be a major, obviously difficult change, or else there's not much point to the story. If her ambition is to win the fireside dancing contest, or to cook the best venison stew, and she gives up those ambitions by the end of the book, then what has she really given up? No, her ambition will clearly need to be much larger than that!

A high-stakes external goal is needed, and it must relate directly to her flaw. What's the biggest ambition I can think up for Pocahontas? If she must give up her ambitions by the end of the book, then what goal will really *sting* when she finally decides to let it go?

Fill in Line 2 in your Story Core with the character's external goal.

1. Main character: Pocahontas, a Native girl of the Powhatan tribe living in 1607.

2. External goal: To become a female chieftain and rule over her own tribe.

3. [blank]

4. [blank]

5. End: Has given up on all ambitions. Sacrificing for her people. Ambiguous.

Flaw: Too driven by ambition. She steps on others in her attempts to attain glory.

You've been able to fill in several points of story and plot just by examining your character's flaw. Now it's time to do more work on the character arc. The coming pages will help you develop a more profound understanding of who your main character is, how serious her flaw is, and exactly how she'll go about pursuing her external goal.

Character Arc: Antagonist

When we read the word "antagonist," many of us get an instant picture in our heads of a classic villain—a "bad guy," whose aim is to stop the main character from achieving his goal using a variety of dastardly tactics. We're so used to thinking of our main characters and their antagonists in this dichotomous sense that in some types of stories, wherein the good/bad dichotomy doesn't exist, we'll have a difficult time identifying just who the antagonist *is*.

Lolita illustrates the idea of a subtle antagonist beautifully, and shows why you can't simply regard your main character's antagonist as a "bad guy." If somebody were to ask you who Humbert Humbert's antagonist is, you might be tempted to say it's Clare Quilty, the *other* creepy child-abuser in the story who pursues Humbert and Lolita across the country, waiting for his chance to snatch Lo from Humbert's clutches. But Quilty is, believe it or not, Humbert's *ally*—at least in the technical sense; in the story-building, outline-creating sense. We'll talk more about allies in the next section.

Humbert's key antagonist is actually Lolita herself. (As in most complex stories, Humbert faces a number of less-important antagonists at different points in the story. But in the overall arc of the story—in his *character* arc—Lolita is his primary opponent.)

How do you determine your character's key antagonist? His external goal will reveal the antagonist to you. *The antagonist is the person who is most heavily invested in achieving the same external goal.* Because this heavily-invested person will struggle just as hard for that one external goal as your character will, they will present the biggest obstacle to your character—they alone, out of all the potential antagonists, will give your character the hardest and most compelling journey.

Humbert's external goal is to possess Lolita—to maintain control of her body and mind. Who wants to maintain control of Lolita's body and mind with just as much fervor—and even more than Quilty wants to control her? Lolita does, of course! Therefore, she is Humbert's key antagonist.

As I mentioned previously, I learned an awful lot from John Truby's book, *The Anatomy of Story*. One of the biggest lessons I took from Truby's method involves antagonists—the part they play not only in the events of the plot, but in the character arc, too. Truby asserts (and I agree with him) that you can't really know your main character until you've got your antagonist figured out—that the antagonist is a crucial cast member who shows you who your protagonist truly is inside, and, more critically, what he could potentially become at the end of his journey. Truby admonishes his readers to spend plenty of time thinking about and developing the antagonist, for your protagonist won't become "real" without a strong-willed, logically behaving antagonist to oppose him.

I'm passing along the same admonishment to you. Just as you can't understand *hot* without knowing what *cold* is, or *dry* without *wet*, so you can't really grasp what motivates your main character—what he's truly after, how deep his flaw runs, and what's at stake for him by the journey's end—until you've provided a clear, logical antagonist whose motives and behaviors make sense within the context of the setting.

Far from being a cape-swishing, mustache-twirling cliché of a villain, your antagonist is a separate individual in her own right, with her own personality and emotional journey (even though you might not explore her character arc in your book.) Because she is her own person, a different reality motivates her, and she will use different tactics than your main character uses. But she wants to achieve the same external goal just as badly.

By using different tactics and motives, your antagonist will act as a sort of "photo negative" or inverse version of your main character. She offers an alternate view to multiple aspects of your book—a subliminal message to the reader that if the main character doesn't overcome his flaw, *this* is at stake. Maybe the tactics your antagonist uses show what a desperate, bad person she's become—and hint that the same fate might befall your protagonist if he's not careful. The antagonist might provide a hint to a "dark side" of your theme—or a "light side," if your theme is already very dark. The antagonist might give some foreshadowing to the book's climax, hinting at the final battle that will decide who wins the external goal. The antagonist might be a warning sign to your main character: "Change your internal flaw, or you'll end up just like me." (Think Darth Vader in the *Star Wars* films.) She might be any of these things, all of them at once, or some other variation on the "photo negative" theme.

But your antagonist is always after the same external goal that your main character pursues, and the antagonist always serves as a symbol to the reader: *here* is the alternate reality, the way things will be (or will remain) if the main character fails to reach his external goal, or if he succeeds in reaching his goal.

Sometimes the *way* in which both characters are chasing the *same* goal isn't immediately obvious. Sometimes, on the surface, they seem to be pursuing *directly opposite* goals. This is often just a matter of how you look at it.

I received an email from a reader that illustrates this point well. He told me that his main character is trying to break a curse that was laid on him by the antagonist, while the antagonist's goal was obviously to keep the curse in place. "How can these two characters possibly be pursuing the same goal?" he asked.

If you look at it as cursed/not cursed, the goals look completely opposite, don't they? But peek at this story from a slightly different perspective and the sameness of their goals suddenly becomes clear. They're vying to *determine the main character's fate*—whether he remains cursed or not. The external goal is control over the main character's reality.

Sometimes making a slight alteration to perspective can clarify whole swaths of story!

(Let me make another interjection, because this seems like a good place to do it: Although I always love receiving reader emails and I'm *beyond* thrilled with how much use folks have gotten from this book, you don't need my approval or my blessing on any aspect of your story. You don't need to run anything by me to get the green light. I'm not some grand authority on story; I'm just a writer like you, and I happened to have a little advice to share, so I shared it. Whatever you want to do with your story, including deviating entirely from the method I am teaching you, is totally fine. I promise. If you're thinking you should run an idea by me to see whether I think it'll hold up in your book, you'll get a more thorough response by asking your friends in your critique group or putting it up for discussion on a writing forum. I guarantee you, my answer will always be "I don't know. Try it and see what happens!" I'm afraid I'm just not very helpful with that sort of thing. I also won't critique your outline or "fix" it for you. I'm way too busy, guys, and you only paid $2.99 for this ebook, or $8.99 for the paperback. That's not enough money to entice me into fixing your story for you. Sorry to disappoint!)

Back to the lesson plan...

Let's look at that "different perspective on the antagonist" idea again, using an example from the canon of literature. In *Lolita*, Humbert's external goal is to possess Lolita. Lolita's external goal is to achieve and maintain autonomy. Looks like different goals on the surface, but when you shift your view just a tad, you can see where they align. They both share a goal of controlling Lolita's fate.

The conflict between them is clear, and the stakes

are high. If Humbert achieves his external goal, Lolita will be forever victimized. If Lolita achieves her goal, she will be free, and Humbert's reality will be shattered. He'll be forced out of his comfortable world of power, selfishness, and vanity, and will face the truth about his own internal flaw.

It's certain that Lolita, a victimized child, is no "bad guy," even though Humbert often tries to paint her as such. This example shows the pitfalls of thinking of your protagonist and antagonist in simplified, good-guy/bad-guy terms. (Though of course, it's perfectly okay if your antagonist really *is* just pure, overwhelming evilness made flesh. Sauron, anyone?)

Since you know your character's flaw and her external goal, you can now determine who will be her most logical antagonist. Take some time to think about the "photo negative" quality of the antagonist's role. Who wants the same external goal, but can reveal an opposite or cautionary aspect to the protagonist and to the reader? Whose different approach to attaining the same goal will serve as an "alternate reality" to your main character and to the reader? That character is your best choice for a dramatic, high-impact antagonist.

Once you have a clear idea of your antagonist, fill in Line 3 of your Story Core. Your outline should now look like this:

1. *Main character: Pocahontas, a Native girl of the Powhatan tribe living in 1607.*

2. *External goal: To become a female chieftain and rule over her own tribe.*

3. *Antagonist: Tribe leaders (first her father, Powhatan—later in the story, her uncle.)*

4. *[blank]*

5. *End: Has given up on all ambitions. Sacrificing for her people. Ambiguous.*

Flaw: Too driven by ambition. She steps on others in her attempts to attain glory.

Character Arc: Ally

The ally is a fascinating part of a well-constructed story—one that is all too often overlooked by writers. Allies are usually so subtle that they're frequently taken for granted by readers, too, and I think that's why many authors fail to include them in their stories, or fail to make full use of the ally.

You might assume that an ally is simply a friend or loved one—a character who's sympathetic to the protagonist's plight, is "on their side," and lends a hand with the plot action when necessary. That's all typically true of ally figures, but their *real* role in story is very specific and is an extremely important part of the character arc.

The ally is the one who *has the power to force the main character onto his correct path*. You'll see in the next few sections, as we begin to "beef up" the outine, that your main character will get sidetracked from the task of fixing his internal flaw. He'll appear to be pursuing his external goal, but really he's running from his inner flaw, afraid to face his weakness.

Your main character has the power to resist change—to put off confronting his flaw even as he reaches for his external goal. But because you gave him an external goal that is intrinsically tied to his flaw, he'll never be able to attain his external goal until he finally confronts his weakness.

It's the ally who will finally turn the plot toward its climax, by backing your character into a corner and forcing him to confront his flaw. The ally is the only character who has the power to do so. The ally is so important to the protagonist that when he finally speaks up, the main character can't help but listen to his voice. The main character can no longer deny that his flaw must be confronted. The ally has forced his hand, for the main character's own good.

Sometimes it can be difficult to identify who the ally actually *is*. The ally might be an obvious friend-type figure, one for whom the main character has clear affection. Or the ally might masquerade in the guise of an antagonist—or might actually *be* a true antagonist at certain points in the story! But it's always the *ally* who finally presents the main character with no further options—who shows him that it's "do or die time," and that now his only real option is to face his inner flaw.

As I mentioned in the previous section, Clare Quilty serves as the ally figure in *Lolita*. It's a bit strange to fathom, because at some points of the story, Quilty is also an antagonist. And since he and Humbert have never liked each other, Quilty makes for a very unlikely ally. Add to this stew of unlikelihood the fact that Qulity only reveals his role as the ally figure when Humbert kills him, and you have an even more unusual ally situation.

Yet Quilty is the one who finally presents Humbert's need to confront his inner flaw in stark, unavoidable terms. And as Humbert has always seen Quilty as a sort of mirror-universe variation on himself, only Quilty has the power to really make Humbert open his eyes.

Allies can be so subtle in a story that they seem totally inactive. Yet they still hold an astounding power to influence the main character's thoughts and actions. Perhaps in your book, your main character used to be the best terrorist-hunter in the world. But he's retired now, and his terrorist-hunting days are behind him. Until, that is, a group of terrorists hold his daughter hostage. In this case, freeing the daughter is obviously his external goal. But the daughter, passive though she may be, also plays the role of the ally. She alone has the power to force your main character to change his actions, confront his weakness, and embark on the journey to win his hero status.

Let's look at some more examples of allies and the power they hold over your main character.

In *Charlotte's Web*, the spider Charlotte plays a more typical ally role. She is a friend to Wilbur all along, and Wilbur has great affection for her. She helps him achieve his external goal, but she shows her real importance when she forces Wilbur to confront his flaw. She tells Wilbur (and I paraphrase, of course,) "I'm going to die. There's nothing you can do about that. You can't put death off forever; you'll have to make peace with it and learn how to handle your grief."

In *Ender's Game* by Orson Scott Card, Ender burns out on his strict school life and loses his motivation. He decides to give up on learning to fight the invading aliens, and chooses instead to enjoy a quiet, secluded life, living by himself in a house on a lake and forgetting all about the intergalactic threat to humanity. He's visited by his sister, Valentine, who is at first sympathetic with him, but soon grows angry with his apathy. She points out that if he doesn't return to school and become a great military commander, *she* will probably be killed by the aliens. "I'm talking about my life, you self-centered little bastard," she says. Valentine is the one person in the world who has the power to back Ender into a corner and force him onto the correct path.

LIBBIE HAWKER

Who is the figure in your book who has that kind of influence over your main character? The ally doesn't need to be a friend or family member—though he might be. The ally doesn't even need to be somebody your character gets along with. But it must be somebody who has the power to force your reluctant character to face his flaw.

Note who your ally is below your character's flaw. Your outline should now look like this:

> *1. Main character: Pocahontas, a Native girl of the Powhatan tribe living in 1607.*
>
> *2. External goal: To become a female chieftain and rule over her own tribe.*
>
> *3. Antagonist: Tribe leaders (first her father, Powhatan—later in the story, her uncle.)*
>
> *4. [blank]*
>
> *5. End: Has given up on all ambitions. Sacrificing for her people. Ambiguous.*

> *Flaw: Too driven by ambition. She steps on others in her attempts to attain glory.*
>
> *Ally: Matachanna, Pocahontas's beloved half-sister.*

Zigging and Zagging Into Theme

You're not done creating your character arc yet, but once I've figured out my antagonist and ally, I always zig-zag off course for a while, and take some time to ruminate on the book's theme. I find it very useful to understand my book's theme before proceeding with the rest of the outline.

I can hear some of you groaning as you read this section. "Great," you're saying. "I have to put a *theme* in my book? Themes are only for that 'high literature' stuff that gets taught in universities, not for my nice, entertaining genre fiction."

Not so, my friend! I contend that theme is not just for literary fiction. I firmly believe that *every* really compelling book has a theme. Theme is a unifying force that keeps a story feeling cohesive and coherent, even though the author might explore a plethora of subplots and take on countless main characters. Theme is, in fact, one of the features that make great books so great.

I know that academics can bloviate endlessly about a book's theme. Since nobody but the author really knows the *true* theme of a book, I find such discussions just as tedious as you probably do. When I talk about theme, I'm not suggesting that you inject some kind of intellectual "higher meaning" into your work. I certainly don't think that deep, academic, bloviation-inducing theme is necessary in *any* book, not even in works of literary fiction.

The kind of theme I'm talking about is simply a *unifying concept*. What outlook on the world, or on human behavior, are you trying to explore? It can be simple and light, without a hint of academic profundity. The theme of *The Cat in the Hat*, for example, is that fun can easily get out of hand. The theme of *Charlotte's Web* is that love transcends death. The theme of *Harry Potter and the Sorcerer's Stone* is that we all must begin to grow into the people we are meant to be. You don't need to read any "layers" or existential truths into these themes. They are merely simple, one-line statements that neatly conceptualize the point of the story.

Think of your theme in the same way. Theme, for the purposes of your outline, isn't layered meaning or a profound truth. It's just a way of boiling down the *point* of your book into one sentence. It's worth putting thought into that one-line concept now, because it will be the yardstick you use to measure the worth of all the ideas you'll try and discard over the next few sections, as you beef up your outline.

I'm going to risk some boos and hisses here, but I'll use my own opinion about the relative merits of two popular works of epic fantasy to illustrate my point about theme.

In my opinion (please don't come after me with pitchforks and torches if you disagree), *A Song of Ice and Fire* by George R. R. Martin is a superb work of literature. It's already up to five volumes and will apparently require at least two more to wrap up the story. The cast of main characters numbers in the dozens, and the subplots are as numerous as the capillaries in your hand. Yet these volumes feel cohesive and relevant to one another, and even after five very large installments, the story continues to compel. Why? Because I can sum up the theme of *ASOIAF* in one simple line: "Even good people will do terrible things in pursuit of power." Every main character's arc, even newly introduced main characters, is an exploration of that same theme.

The Wheel of Time series by Robert Jordan and Brandon Sanderson stands in stark contrast to *ASOIAF*...**in my opinion**. *Wheel of Time* seems to have started out with a unifying theme—a very simplistic "Good should triumph over evil." However, as the series expanded across its fourteen volumes, that rather vague and general theme wasn't enough to corral all of Jordan's ideas. As a means of measuring which scenes to include and which to discard, "Good should triumph over evil" hasn't proven very effective. *WoT*, as a consequence, feels bloated and far too drawn-out, with plenty of scenes that feel extraneous and irrelevant.

A more specific theme, or closer attention paid to the *importance* of theme, could have kept *WoT* relatively trim, undeniably tighter, and far more compelling than it turned out to be. **In my opinion**. (Seriously, I can feel some of you forming an angry mob already. And Brandon Sanderson, if you read this book, I think you did an absolutely *brilliant* job bringing an out-of-control series to a logical and satisfying close. You are a hero for accomplishing that feat, as far as I'm concerned.)

Let the examples of *ASOIAF* and *WoT* be a lesson to you: theme can make or break your book, and it will almost certainly decide how efficient your outline is—how quickly you can take a book from outline to completed draft.

Theme serves as one of your most useful guide posts. It is your handy-dandy measuring tape, allowing you to quickly assess ideas for their utility. Theme-as-guidepost will allow you to quickly discard scenes or concepts that don't bear directly on the *point* of your book, which in turn will give you the ability to cut away dead wood and shed extraneous scenes *now*, in the outlining phase, and not *later*, after you've already written 30,000 pointless words that are just going to be discarded in edits.

I speak from experience here: my first novel, *The Sekhmet Bed*, was 120,000 words long when I finished the first draft, but 90,000 words long when I finally published it. I spent (wasted, you might say) a lot of time writing those 30,000 deleted words. A well-chosen, specific theme would have prevented me from dawdling away all those hours on unused words. A well-chosen and specific theme can also prevent you from creating a bloated, shambling book or series that lumbers awkwardly along with no end in sight.

I know that sometimes it's hard to discern a theme at such an early stage. It will make the outlining process much easier if you can identify your theme now, but if you're really struggling terribly with it, you can leave the theme alone for the moment.

In fact, you might even be able to ignore theme entirely until you've finished your final draft! On occasion, that has happened to me. But by the time you've finished writing your book, an obvious theme should have asserted itself. If you've gotten all the way through a first draft and the point of your book is still a total mystery to you, then the lack of a cohesive theme is probably an indicator of a broken story. Somewhere, something isn't adding up. You'll need to re-examine your outline—the bones of your story—looking critically at how your character's flaw, Story Core, plot, and pacing relate. If no clear theme has emerged, you may have a selfish, vain Harry Potter facing leadership trials that have nothing to do with his internal flaw.

However, if you look hard enough, I bet you can probably see a theme clearly at this point in the game, and identifying it *now* will make the writing process much easier. Remember that theme doesn't have to be a "big idea." It's just the overarching concept that unifies your story.

For example, the theme of *Tidewater* is "Exploring three different ways people might respond to the same cultural clash." (Remember, although I've been using just Pocahontas's character outline in my examples so far, *Tidewater* actually has three main characters, each with his or her own arc/outline.) As you can see, I'm not going into any academic contortions over theme. I'm not trying to inject profundity into my book. I'm simply stating what the *point* is—what frames the window through which the reader will gaze onto the world of *Tidewater*.

Maybe the theme of a romance novel is "We're stronger together than we are apart." A sci-fi adventure might have the theme of "Bravery and ingenuity can conquer adversity." You might describe the theme of *A Clockwork Orange* as "Even criminals deserve free will," and *The Great Gatsby* as "The American dream isn't all it's cracked up to be."

So spend some time thinking about your book. What's the setting going to be like? How old is your ideal audience? What flaw have you chosen for your character, and what does your interest in such a flaw say about your outlook on the world? What point are you trying to make by exploring this particular flaw? How does this character's journey reflect your beliefs or interests? All of these questions will help you identify your theme.

When you've got it, add it below the "ally" entry in your outline. If you haven't figured out the theme yet, leave a blank space there and move on to the next section, but keep one eye open for your theme. It could make itself known to you at any time.

Your outline should now look like this:

1. Main character: Pocahontas, a Native girl of the Powhatan tribe living in 1607.

2. External goal: To become a female chieftain and rule over her own tribe.

3. Antagonist: Tribe leaders (first her father, Powhatan—later in the story, her uncle.)

4. [blank]

5. End: Has given up on all ambitions. Sacrificing for her people. Ambiguous.

Flaw: Too driven by ambition. She steps on others in her attempts to attain glory.

Ally: Matachanna, Pocahontas's beloved half-sister.

Theme: Exploring three different ways people might respond to a cultural clash.

Plot: Begin to Spin

There's only one blank space now in your Story Core: Line 4, which will become the "meat" of your plot. Now we're going to spin the sequential events of your plot, and together, they'll make up the concept that fits into Line 4 of your Story Core.

You'll recall that near the beginning of this book, I said that plot can change dramatically, even while the three legs of your outline (character arc, theme, and pacing) and your Story Core remain exactly the same. You'll begin to see what I mean by that in this section.

Think of your plot—the sequential, "external" events of your book—as a physical structure that supports your main character's journey. Visualize the plot-structure as a bridge stretching from Point A to Point B. That bridge is made out of three kinds of bricks, and each brick is made from character arc, theme, or Story Core. You can rearrange those bricks however you please, but you will only use bricks from those three sources. Depending on how you arrange the bricks, your bridge might have any variety of appearances. It could be smooth and direct, or it could peak and valley like a roller coaster. It might be straight, or it might arch in the middle. You might construct it one way, decide you don't like it, tear it down and re-assemble an entirely new structure. The appearance of the bridge ultimately doesn't matter. What matters is that it spans from Point A to Point B, and that it's assembled only with bricks made of character arc, theme, and Story Core.

Line 4 of your outline represents the character's journey—her attempt to achieve her external goal. Line 4 is also the path that will lead your character to Line 5—that is, her success or failure with regards to the external goal, and also her success or failure with regards to her inner flaw.

Now we're going to spin our plot—build that A-to-B brickwork bridge—to fill the Line 4 gap.

Add some entries below the "theme" line. Put in another line break first, so you've got a little visual "blank space" before the meat of your outline, and label the new lines with the following headings:

Opening Scene

Inciting Event

Character Realizes External Goal

Display of Flaw

Drive for Goal

Antagonist Revealed

Thwart #1

Revisiting Flaw

New Drive for Goal

Antagonist Attacks

Thwart #2

Changed Goal

Ally Attacks

Girding the Loins

Battle

Death

Outcome

This, as you've probably guessed, will become the outline for the bulk of your story—the guide for the actual sentences, paragraphs, and scenes you'll create. Your task is now to fill in the specifics, sketching out scenes that correspond with each heading. The headings represent the typical components of a mythic hero's journey, and will guarantee a story that feels complete and dramatic. I'll walk you through each heading, explaining its necessity and giving examples where warranted.

But as you read up on each part of the plot outline, you must remember that you can only build this bridge with bricks taken from your established character arc, theme, and Story Core. If you're tempted to sketch in a scene that has nothing to do with your theme, or isn't taken from part of your Story Core, discard it. Save that scene for a future work. Because you've spent so much time developing the relationship between character arc, theme, and Core, you already know that any scene which doesn't relate to any of those three elements simply doesn't belong in this book.

Remember: Harry Potter's flaw (brick: character arc) is that he's too meek and hasn't learned how to be a leader. If you were J.K. Rowling (don't we all wish) and you were writing the outline for *Harry Potter and the Sorcerer's Stone*, would you introduce a scene where Harry is forced to confront his own selfishness or vanity? Of course not; that has nothing to do with his flaw. Such a scene would feel irrelevant to the story.

Humbert Humbert's external goal is to retain control of Lolita (brick: Story Core.) If you were Vladimir Nabokov, outlining *Lolita*, would you write a scene where Humbert tries to win an Academy Award? Of course not; that has nothing to do with your main character's established goal.

If you were E.B. White outlining *Charlotte's Web*, would you include an ending where Wilbur discovers a magical elixir that makes all his friends live forever, so no one ever has to die or experience grief? Of course not! That scene would clash with your unifying idea that love transcends death (brick: theme.) That scene would also allow Wilbur to shirk his duty to grow as a person (brick: character arc.) Unless he confronts his flaw, Wilbur can't emerge at the end of his story with hero status, and your readers won't feel very satisfied by that outcome.

Keep these examples in mind as you learn about each part of the plot outline (I refer to each one as a "heading") and consider carefully how you'll use your three sources of building-bricks to fill out each heading.

As you fill in your plot headings, keep your entries for each one broad and loose. You'll tighten and refine each idea when we get to the "pacing" section of this book. For now, staying loose and general with your ideas will probably be more useful than getting really specific.

If you're working on an outline for a book with more than one main character, create a complete outline for each main character, including the plot headings. In each separate character's plot headings, include scenes and plot points that bear *only on their personal journey and external goals*, just as if they were the only "star" in your book. I'll help you determine whether multiple characters are truly "main" characters, and therefore worthy of their own outlines, in a later section of this book. Then I'll show you how to weave multiple completed outlines together into a single, larger outline for one multi-protagonist book.

For now, though, read through all the parts of the plot headings thoroughly, so you know what kind of work lies ahead. Then you can fill in the headings on your outline.

Plot: Opening Scene

I hardly have to tell you that the opening scene will set your book's stage. It should introduce your world, elegantly and cleanly, with action relevant to the main character, not with an unattached "info dump." It should give a clear idea of when and where this story takes place, and what your main character is like in general terms.

I also like to take the opening scene as an opportunity to address either the character's flaw or the theme. Sometimes you can fit both in without any obvious contortions.

Showing the reader a clear view of flaw or theme right up front, in the first few pages of your book, sets a strong subconscious hook. It gives an immediate impression that there will be a major problem explored in this story—it won't just be a rambling pastiche where nothing happens, except for a lot of navel-gazing. Make the reader sense straight away that a hero's journey lies ahead.

To develop the specifics of your opening scene, think about your character's Point A—their flaw. Eventually they'll struggle to get to Point B—a higher state. But right now, they're low-down. How can you show that their situation isn't ideal, either externally or internally?

Or, consider how you can provide an initial illustration of the book's theme. For example, in the opening scene of *Charlotte's Web* a little girl saves a runty piglet, Wilbur, from an early death—thus setting up the theme of love transcending death, which pervades the entire story.

Plot: Inciting Event

The inciting event is something that happens to boot your character out of his everyday reality. It must make him look around at his present state and decide that soemthing isn't quite right. Maybe he's starting to get an inkling of his flaw, but hasn't yet fully realized how deeply flawed he is. Or maybe he sees his external goal for the first time. Occasionally the inciting event corresponds with the opening scene, but sometimes it takes a scene or two before your character's real incitement appears.

In *Harry Potter and the Sorcerer's Stone*, the inciting event is when Harry receives his invitations to enroll at Hogwarts. This occurrence awakens him to the fact that a parallel magical world exists alongside the "Muggle" world, and that his destiny is to become a part of it.

The inciting event is almost always closely tied to your character's external goal.

Plot: Character Realizes External Goal

Sometimes the character's realization of his external goal is exactly the same as the inciting event, but not always. If in your story the two plot points do not overlap, sketch in the scene where your main character first decides that he will in fact go after his external goal.

In *Lolita*, the inciting event is the scene where Humbert sees Lolita for the first time, sunbathing on the piazza. But he doesn't realize his external goal—to make Lolita his plaything—until the afternoon when they both skip church and have a very peculiar encounter on the sofa. At that point, Humbert knows that he is committed to pursuing his goal, even though it's criminal and he knows what danger he could lead himself into.

Plot: Display of Flaw

Your character might have displayed his flaw as early as the opening scene. If he hasn't yet made his flaw known to the reader, make it known now, so that it's established early in the book.

Clear establishment of the flaw will put tension on the hook you've already set into your reader. If the reader understands early on that this characer is in need of personal change, then the reader understands that this is a book with a hero's journey—one that will follow expected and familiar patterns; a book that is likely to deliver a satisfying ending.

You might think it's better to prove to your reader that your book is unlike anything else out there— that this is a totally unique reading experience that doesn't have any similarity to any other story. I hate to break it to you, but that's a losing game. Even readers who *think* they only want to read 100%

original fiction, totally unlike anything else that's ever been done before, are mistaken. The human mind is drawn like a magnet to established story patterns. That's why the "hero's journey" pattern of ancient myth has persisted throughout all of human history. (And it's also why Hollywood has been endlessly rehashing the same characters and stories for the past twenty years. Familiarity sells. Frustrating, but true.)

By making it very clear in the earliest scenes that your character is in need of personal growth, you are lighting up a big, blinking, neon sign that says to the reader's subconscious, "Good Book!" Your assurance of familiarity and predictable outcomes at this point will not chase readers away, but will reel them in closer.

As they read, they'll find delight in the unique spin you put on the old familiar narrative pattern. You might even surprise them later, by deviating dramatically from the expected path. We all remember the furor on the internet when readers found out what happens to Ned Stark in George R. R. Martin's *A Game of Thrones*. Save deviations and surprise twists for later, when the reader is thoroughly hooked. For now, provide the comfort and lure of familiarity. Predictability at this early stage is a strong incentive to keep reading.

Typically the best way to establish the flaw for the *reader's* benefit is to show the flaw *in action*, having some serious impact on another character. "Show" the main character's flaw at work; don't just "tell" the reader about it.

Plot: Drive for Goal

You have now established that your main character has a clear need for personal growth, has his eye on an external goal, and has realized that he would, in fact, like to strive toward that goal. You've just clearly signaled to the reader that this is no rambly pastiche; you have promised a complete and compelling story with a satisfying ending.

Now it's time to dive into the meaty, juicy action.

I learned much about the effectiveness (and the incredible ubiquity) of the formula I'm about to describe from John Truby's aforementioned book, *The Anatomy of Story*. For an in-depth study of why this particular construction feels so psychologically gripping to audiences, I recommend you read Truby's book. But for now, trust me: follow this pattern and your plot will feel as tight as a drum head.

Your character will now make his first attempt to reach his external goal. Remember: since his external goal is tied to his flaw, and he hasn't yet overcome his flaw, he won't be able to reach his goal on the first attempt. *He must achieve his personal growth and complete the hero's journey before he can get his hands on the ultimate prize.*

At this stage, give your character an ill-fated plan. He's definitely moving toward his goal, but he won't succeed. Brainstorm some plausible events that might fit the bill. Consider these factors as you brainstorm this initial drive toward the goal:

His plan must make sense within the context of the setting. For example, having him use magic if you haven't already established that magic exists in this universe would just be implausible and weird.

This initial attempt should show the reader how his flaw still holds him back. This will cement in the reader's mind that the character's internal journey is ultimately more important than the quest for the external goal. The character might not yet realize that his inner flaw is holding him back, but that fact should be reasonably clear to the reader.

Ideally, the attempt should relate to the theme in some obvious way.

If you can involve the ally in a meaningful way, without stretching credibility too far, then that can also serve you well later on.

Plot: Antagonist Revealed

You already know that the antagonist is one of the most important characters in your book. He provides an imposing obstacle to your main character, and thus ensures plenty of drama and tension. It's the antagonist's "realness" that makes that key moment when the main character finally conquers his flaw so fulfilling.

The antagonist isn't only important for dramatic reasons. He is also crucial because he offers a different way of seeing the world—a different lens through which the reader can examine the theme. The antagonist is an alternate reality, a cautionary tale, or a fork in the road.

A character this important deserves a great scene. Really think about how you'll introduce him. Rather than simply making him a cartoonish villain, do your best to humanize him. If he is obviously a fully developed individual, and not a cliché "bad guy," then his opposition to the main character will carry so much more meaning, and affect the reader much more deeply. A well-developed antagonist, deployed properly into your plot, is one of your best assurances that your book will surely be a good one.

In the "antagonist revealed" stage, sometimes you're revealing the antagonist as an entirely new character—someone who wasn't present in the story until this point. Sometimes you're revealing that an already-present character is taking on the role of the antagonist. Whichever path your story calls for, treat your antagonist with care and respect. As the "photo negative" of your main character, he could have *been* your main character if his path through life had been just a little bit different.

The antagonist's reason for opposing the main character should be logical, a natural progression from events in his own life. If you simply stuff in a "bad guy" at this point because the plot calls for it, then the main character's struggle and emotional growth will have little meaning for the reader. Your main character will simply be swinging his sword at a straw man, and scenes between the two characters will lack a sense of urgency or peril.

The antagonist has to want that goal as badly as your main character does. Show the reader *why* he wants it.

Plot: Thwart #1

Your main character hasn't even come close yet to conquering his flaw and completing his personal growth. Since you developed his external goal by evaluating his internal flaw, that goal is specifically tailored to hang out of his reach until he has confronted his need for change. In short: there's no way he can get what he wants so easily.

Here is where you must decide how and why he's thwarted. Sometimes it's because the antagonist has also made a bid for the external goal, and has pushed the main character farther away, or pushed him off course. Sometimes the "antagonist revealed" and "thwart #1" steps are one and the same, with your antagonist becoming known to the main character in the same moment that he meets defeat. Occasionally, the event has little to do with the antagonist, and appears to be a matter of fate (but is in reality a matter of your book's theme.)

In *Charlotte's Web*, the little girl, Fern, saves baby Wilbur from the axe. Wilbur grows up to love barnyard life, and certainly wants to go on enjoying it. (External goal: stay alive.) But when he grows too large for the family's farm, he is moved to the farm of Homer Zuckerman, Fern's uncle. There he'll have plenty of room to grow... big and plump and juicy! It's the move to the new farm that represents the first thwart in Wilbur's story, and Homer Zuckerman is his antagonist— the character who also wants to decide whether Wilbur lives or dies. In this case, the first thwart and the antagonist appear at the same time, and the first thwart has more to do with "fate" (theme) than with any direct action by the antagonist. But you can see how the thwart relates directly to the book's theme, and how the antagonist is involved even if he's not directly responsible.

Plot: Revisiting the Flaw

Now that your character has experienced some disappointment, you get to rub his face in his failure. After all, he hasn't yet confronted his internal flaw. He's resisting his duty to embark on the true hero's journey and fix what's broken inside him. This calls for a stern lesson!

Here, you'll show the character's flaw again, so it's clear to the reader that his failure to confront his flaw directly is the real source of his troubles. I usually find it useful at this point to begin sowing the seeds of self-doubt in the character's mind. At this stage, I often introduce the character's first inkling that maybe he's not as flawless as he thought, and that perhaps some change is warranted.

But he's not quite ready to give up his old ways yet...

Plot: New Drive for the Goal

The main character makes a new plan to reach his goal. A bit more cautious now, thanks to his brief moment of introspection, and perhaps wary of the antagonist or other forces, he is just as motivated as ever to claim that external prize, but because he still refuses to own up to his failings and affect a change, it continues to dangle out of his reach.

Plot: Antagonist Attacks

The character has just begun to soften and examine his own behavior a little bit. Now is the perfect time to spring a strong attack from his antagonist. If it wasn't clear to the main character already, the events of this plot point make it clear to him that "fate" isn't behind his failures. He has an antagonist—somebody else is driving toward his coveted prize. The prize just got even more desirable.

Sometimes it's wonderful fun to set characters up as if they're allies, but to surprise the reader (and the main character) by revealing that they're actually antagonists—either the key antagonist who will ultimately confront the main character at his most vulnerable moment of change, or minor antagonists who needle and plague him in subplots. You can create as many offshoot attacks by secret/surprise antagonists as you please, but don't neglect to build these subplots with the same bricks you're using to construct your main outline. Keep everything focused on the same character arc, Core, or theme, and even your subplots will feel cohesive.

Plot: Thwart #2

...But sadly for your main character, because he hasn't yet accepted his need for change, he just can't win. He is thwarted again—this time, clearly by his antagonist.

Your main character now knows that his antagonist is powerful and driven. The external goal looks more out of his reach than ever before.

It's important to note here that you can add in as many drive toward goal/antagonist attacks/main character thwarted sequences as you'd like. You don't have to stick to the number I suggest; they can keep on going for dozens of rounds if you'd like. The key to making repeated drive/attack/thwart sequences feel relevant and not repetitive is to slowly increase the main character's self-awareness with each thwart. Each time, his eyes are opened a little wider to the antagonist's potency and his own inadequacy, until finally, he can no longer deny that his inner flaw is the source of his woes.

Plot: Changed Goal

Because his external goal now seems so very out of reach, your character changes his course entirely. He gives up on the external goal, or shifts his focus to a different external goal that is barely related.

Now we have a real problem, don't we? The whole point of a story is to watch a character go through emotional growth, and you selected the character's external goal specifically to lure him into a confrontation with his inner flaw. If he goes chasing off after another goal now, you'll lose him! He might never confront his need for change, and then he'll never achieve his hero status!

When you create the changed goal for your main character, be sure it's logical and has some ties to the other elements of your story. Remember, you can only build this bridge out of bricks taken from character arc, Story Core, and theme. He has a new external goal now, and is ready to cede the original goal to the antagonist—but his new goal must still relate in some way to the remainder of your story.

In *Lolita*, after Lo gives Humbert the slip and disappears, Humbert tries to track her down for a while. But when he realizes it's an impossible task, he takes up with a new girlfriend, Rita. Rita is a grown woman, but she has some childlike qualities that remind him of Lolita—his original external goal. He embarks on a rambling car trip with Rita, which reflects the travels he's already made with Lo. Certain characteristics of Rita and of the car trip keep Humbert's new goal closely tied to prior elements of the narrative, and thus the diversion of Rita still feels relevant to the story overall.

Plot: The Ally Attacks

In the sections dealing with character arc, we discussed the importance of the ally. We learned that the ally is the one character who has the absolute power to force the main character onto the correct path, tearing him from the diversion of his new goal (which, after all, will not cause him to confront his flaw.)

Here, after your main character has given in to the tempting distraction of an barely-related goal, is where your ally must launch her attack. Using her great influence over the main character, she makes him look deep into a mirror and truly face what he sees there. It's the ally who finally smacks the main character upside the head until he acknowledges that he is the cause of all his own troubles and failures. In this scene, the ally must give the main character no choice but to see that he *must* correct his flaw.

You don't have to place the Changed Goal and Attack by Ally here. You can position these plot headings elsewhere in the stream of Drive to Goal/Attack by Antagonist/Thwart headings. You will create a different feel to your narrative depending on where you position this heading.

My genius friend (and fellow author) Cidney Swanson pointed out to me that placing the Changed Goal/Attack by Ally sequence early in the book—say, after Thwart #1—will change the way the reader feels about your main character. Cidney asserts that if you place the Attack by Ally early in the book, the reader will see the character "in abject misery," to use Cidney's words, for much longer—and therefore will feel more sympathy with the reader.

If you place the Changed Goal/Attack by Ally sequence later, as I have suggested here, the reader will feel see the character in need of fixing their flaw for longer, and will feel more tension to witness that change finally come about. The character may be more difficult to like if you place this sequence later, but the change can feel much more gratifying when it's finally made.

Where you place the Changed Goal/Attack by Ally sequence depends on how you want the reader to feel about your character, and what kind of atmosphere you want to give the entire story. As long as it happens before the final battle with the antagonist, though, you can't go wrong.

Plot: Girding the Loins

A less archaic heading for this scene might be "Final Drive" or "Renewed Focus," but I have always loved the phrase "girding the loins." I always use it when I write my own outlines, so here it is, gracing my book.

It's time to gird up your main character's loins. No more screwing around; now he's *really* going to battle—and this time, he's in it to win it.

The confrontation with the almighty ally was just what your main character needed. He is humbled now, gives up on his new, false goal, and finds in himself a will he never knew he had before.

He decides in this scene that he will renew his pursuit of the original external goal—and he acknowledges that he must confront the powerful antagonist in order to do it. The main character is under no illusions now. He knows how deeply flawed he is. He knows that the antagonist is probably more powerful than he is; this will not be an easy fight. He knows that he may not succeed. But because of the ally's influence, he has seen the light. He is ready to face his flaw, to conquer it if he can, and finally win his prize.

What can you write that will show his changed mental state? Sometimes it's a quietly introspective scene where he reflects on his past and knows that those days are behind him. Sometimes it's a dramatic scene where he makes a symbolic sacrifice. Sometimes it can be conveyed more subtly, through imagery: a beautiful sunrise breaks over the distant hills; birds begin to sing in the treetops.

Whatever you choose, make it clear to the reader that the main character has reached his awakening. His feet are firmly on the hero's path now, and he won't stop until his journey comes to its rightful, hard-won end, whatever that end may be.

Plot: The Battle

At last, the main character squares off openly with the antagonist. They strive for the external goal, but of course the reader knows that the main character is really striving to conquer his flaw and achieve his hidden goal: personal growth.

The "battle" scene doesn't have to be a literal battle, of course. It's simply a confrontation with the antagonist, and it must come after the main character has girded up his loins. Since he's done his girding, he gets awfully close to winning the external goal. But the battle isn't yet won...

Plot: "Death"

The "death" is usually the most impactful scene in the book. But don't worry—a literal death isn't necessary (though sometimes you'll find that a literal death has the greatest dramatic value.)

What *dies* in the "death" scene is the character's flaw. In the midst of his final battle with the antagonist, the main character reaches deep within himself and finds the strength to conquer his flaw. He effectively "kills off" the person he was before—a person whose life was controlled by his inner brokenness. Now he has the chance to emerge as a whole, relatively flawless being.

This is the scene when the main character makes the final thrust with his sword, the final sprint to the finish line. With one last, desperate, painful effort, he *grows*. (Or... he doesn't! But he *does* try, even if he fails.) It's the great climax of your book, so make it memorable. Make it count.

Typically, the "death" will involve a dramatic sacrifice. The main character will make some grand, symbolic gesture to show that he is a totally different person now. The sacrifice is a signal to the reader that the old version of the main character is gone for good, and the new version is here to stay, with his hard-won hero status intact.

Plot: Outcome

Here you are, at the end of the plot! Did it really come together as easily as that?

Now you must decide on the final scenes. Look back at your Story Core. Did you decide to give the character a hard, soft, or ambiguous lesson? That decision will guide you in sketching out the basics of this last scene.

The final segment of your book should make it clear whether the character won or lost his external goal. We already know that he managed to win his inner battle, conquer his flaw, and attain hero status. Now all that remains is for us to understand the aftermath of the great battle with the antagonist.

Show who ultimately won the external prize, and spend some time reflecting on the implications of your character's arc. Theme is your unifying concept, so one last revisitation of the book's theme in the final sentences will offer a satisfying sense of closure and cohesion.

A Sketched-In Outline

It might be useful for you to see what my outlines look like at this stage, before I begin refining each scene with beats and pacing. I hope you take note of how general and "loose" the concepts are. Before you apply pacing to your outline, you'll want to keep your ideas flexible and open to creative interpretation.

And *here's* a great place to note that if you're the type of writer who likes to leave much of your book open-ended, available for you to discover *as you write it*, this is where your outlining work ends. You've laid down very rough ideas that will guide you surely to a quality finished product, but the specifics of much of your story are still unknown. With your rough outline as a guide, you can let your creativity run wild and still be assured of a good book when you reach "The End."

However, if you want to maximize the efficiency of your writing time, I recommend you proceed on to learn about pacing. It's the stage of the outline that comes right after you've roughed in each plot heading, and if you want to complete a book with maximum speed, it's essential to work out the pacing of your scenes before you begin to write.

I've mentioned before that my novel *Tidewater* has three main characters. This is the sketched-in outline for Pocahontas's portion of the story—just the initial outline and the roughly defined plot headings. I hope it provides an example of what a filled-in outline looks like at this stage.

1. Main character: Pocahontas, a Native girl of the Powhatan tribe living in 1607.

2. External goal: To become a female chieftain and rule over her own tribe.

3. Antagonist: Tribe leaders (first her father, Powhatan—later in the story, her uncle.)

4. SEE BELOW (Remember, the plot headings are your Line 4.)

5. End: Has given up on all ambitions. Sacrificing for her people. Ambiguous.

Flaw: Too driven by ambition. She steps on others in her attempts to attain glory.

Ally: Matachanna, Pocahontas's beloved

half-sister.

Theme: Exploring three different ways people might respond to a cultural clash.

<u>Opening Scene:</u> *Preparing for a feast, she shirks her duties and angers Matachanna.*

<u>Inciting Event:</u> *Given as handmaid to a high-born relative; dissatisfied with her lot in life.*

<u>Character Realizes External Goal:</u> *Sees female chieftain arrive; clearly wants to be a chieftain herself.*

<u>Display of Flaw:</u> *Behaves cruelly to the girl she's now serving as handmaid; continues to shirk her duties and dumps her chores on her sister.*

<u>Drive for Goal:</u> *When the white men arrive, she makes herself useful as an interpreter so her father will take note of her and give her more status.*

<u>Antagonist Revealed:</u> *Her father Powhatan gets ultimate say over who does what with the white men.*

<u>Thwart #1:</u> *Powhatan places Naukaquawis in charge of monitoring the white men.*

Revisiting Flaw: Angry over this turn of events, she runs off and leaves Matachanna with all the chores again.

New Drive for Goal: Barges into longhouse and asserts herself as interpreter.

Antagonist Attacks: After Pocahontas works successfully as interpreter, Powhatan gets cold feet about the white men and takes a more hard-lined stance with them.

Thwart #2: Pocahontas is forced to negotiate for guns; good relations she's worked hard to establish are destroyed.

New Drive for Goal: Suggests building a garden for the white men to keep them reliant on the Natives.

Antagonist Attacks: John Smith (minor antagonist) allows conflict to erupt over the garden.

Thwart #3: Naukaquawis taken hostage; Pocahontas in deep trouble.

New Drive for Goal: Tries to negotiate with nearby territory to get Naukaquawis freed.

Antagonist Attacks: Powhatan not happy about this; he calls off all contact with white men.

Thwart #4: Proclamation issued that anyone who contacts white men will be killed.

New Drive for Goal: Pocahontas attempts to achieve the high status she wants by participating in an important ceremony at the temple.

Antagonist Attacks: Starving white men attack the temple; temple is burned; Opechancanough (new primary antagonist) declares all-out war on white men.

Thwart #5: Powhatan moves everybody to Orapax (far from the white men.)

Changed Goal: Pocahontas decides to settle into a quiet life as wife to Kocoum.

Ally Attacks: Matachanna blames Pocahontas's involvement with the white men for the move to Orapax; tells her that her ambition makes her too selfish and that she doesn't want to have a relationship with her anymore.

Girding the Loins: In her coming of age ceremony, Pocahontas renounces all ambition before her god and asks for a humble and useful spirit.

Battle: *Kidnapped by the white men; held hostage; she now sees how large the settlement has grown, and that somebody has to act as a bridge between the two cultures or the Natives will be destroyed. Tells Opechancanough (new primary antagonist) that she will marry a white man, with or without his blessing.*

Death: *She accepts baptism so that she may continue living among/learning about the English. Dons English clothing as a symbol of her sacrifice. She is now fully committed to service to her people instead of selfish ambition.*

Outcome: *She becomes a useful tool, serving her people, but she wishes for her son (half-English) to live out his life as a Native, not as an Englishman—thus showing that her heart is still with her people.*

You can see that this outline is still quite loose and rough. The key points of each plot heading are sketched in, but there is little or no detail, no expounding on what exactly happens with each turn of the plot.

That all comes next, as we discuss pacing.

Pacing: The Shape of a Good Book

Every good book has the same shape. I'm not talking about trim size, of course, or hardback versus paperback versus ebook. I'm talking about the book's pace.

That may seem like a bold or even ignorant statement on the surface. When I say that only well-paced books are "good," you might think I'm saying that only action-packed books with lots of frenetic scenes are good, and to heck with anything more languid or cerebral. But that's not what I'm saying at all. A book with tons of action scenes can be poorly paced. Its *true* action—the character arc—can be lost in a whirlwind of unconnected car chases and irrelevant explosions and pointlessly rampaging T-Rexes. Yet a story in which the main character never leaves her room can keep you on the edge of your seat, flipping pages at breakneck speed.

If you've followed my instructions and sketched

out your plot using only elements of character arc, theme, and Story Core, you won't have to worry about irrelevant action. I can guarantee you that all your T-Rex rampages will have a point. But you do need to pay close attention to your story's pace as you expand your outline by embellishing scenes.

Every good narrative—every well-paced book—has exactly the same shape. It doesn't matter whether it's an adventure or a romance or a picture book or a memoir. If it compels the reader to keep on reading, I promise you that you'll find the same shape in its structure.

A good book is shaped like an inverted triangle. It stands on its pointed tip—that's the climax of the book—with its widest side up toward the sky. The wide side of the triangle is the book's opening scene.

In the beginning, there's a lot of "wiggle room" in the story—lots of space to move around up in the wide side of that triangle. Nothing is firmly established yet. You're just being introduced to the character and the world; the plot might go off in any direction.

But as your character sets his eyes on his external goal, the walls of the triangle slowly begin to squeeze him. Your character is being ushered onto an increasingly narrow path, moving inevitably toward the skinny end of the triangle. Soon the traingle's walls press in on him, and there's no escape. As the walls squeeze, he moves faster and more directly toward the triangle's point.

That squeeze, which produces speed, direct movement, and a focus on the story's climax, is your book's pace. Fortunately, if you've followed my instructions, you've already got an inverted triangle laid out in your outline. A tight pace is built reliably into this method, even if your story has a quiet, easy mood.

But of course, there's still some work to be done. Your outline at this stage is only a loose sketch, with general ideas for your chapters and scenes.

Now your task becomes a little more difficult, I'm afraid. You need to refine and define your loose sketch, pumping it up until you have a clear vision of each chapter and scene in your book.

In this process, it's easy to lose sight of your book's overall pace. Now that you have the creative license to start defining actual *scenes*, you might be tempted to put in irrelevant content. If you've already decided that your main character has a fabulous spoon collection, don't give in to the temptation to write a scene wherein he admires his prized souvenirs, *and nothing else happens*.

If a scene doesn't have that inverted-triangle shape, then your pace will be broken. Breaking pace is a sure way to lose your reader's interest—in fact, I'd guess that most readers abandon books because pacing flags once too often. Readers might not even be aware of *why* they lose interest in a book, but if you read critical reviews carefully, you can see that usually shoddy pace is the culprit. Statements like "Nothing happens," or "The character does confusing things," or "I kept finding my attention drifting off" will clue you in to a pacing issue.

On the flip side of the coin, recently I checked out a new and popular historical novel just to see what all the buzz was about. I found absolutely everything about it to be abysmal: the writing style was sophomoric, the events of the plot were silly, the dialog was wooden, the history mangled beyond all recognition, and the characters were cardboard cut-outs with all the depth of a rapidly evaporating puddle. It was *terrible*—and yet I read it all the way through to the end, because the pacing was pitch-perfect. Believe it or not, *I even bought the sequel*, knowing full well that it would be just as bad as the first book—and that I would get just as much enjoyment out of it!

Now you begin to see, I think, why I include pacing in the Three-Legged Outline—why it's just as important as character arc and Story Core. In a very real way, your book's pace will determine its success. If you can be certain at the outline stage that your book has a tight pace, you can be confident that it will pull a reader from opening scene to final scene with ease.

Remember: if a reader can easily make the decision to put your book down, she might never pick it up again. A tight pace has nothing to do with explosions or car chases. It has everything to do with creating a compulsion to keep on reading, even when your reader has other things she really ought to be doing.

It might seem like an impossible task, to plan a reliable pace for your book before you've even begun writing it. But don't worry! I've got a foolproof method that will make it happen—and it will make fleshing out your outline, defining all your chapters and scenes, a snap.

Pacing: Triangles All the Way Down

Many years ago, when I first started getting serious about my writing (and long before I'd ever read a book *about* writing) I discovered something special about the shape of good stories. I observed that every book that kept me glued to its pages had the general inverted-triangle shape that applied to its overall, foundational structure. But what was more interesting to me was that the exact same shape was echoed in each of its chapters, and even in scenes within chapters.

I realized that *a compelling story is always made of a series of nested, inverted triangles.* The overall structure repeats throughout the narrative: broad, flexible opening scene that leads to a "squeeze," which pushes the character inevitably toward a mini-climax at the triangle's point. The point of one triangle spills the character out into the broad opening of a new scene, which ushers him into a new squeeze, then to a new mini-climax, and so on.

This was quite a revelation to me, and I thought I'd made a breakthrough in creative writing theory, until I read exactly that same description years later in John Truby's book. (Yes, I'm referencing Truby's book again. You really ought to read it! And no, I'm not affiliated with Truby or his book in any way. I'm just an author who has benefitted from his knowledge.) I just about jumped for joy when I saw the same explanation of story pacing right there on his pages. I hadn't made an academic breakthrough with my "discovery," but I was *right*. The confirmation of my long-held suspicion was before my eyes. Truby backed me up: tight pace is indeed a series of funnel-like events, broad at the beginning and skinny at the climax, each one leading logically into the next.

You know that a Story Core—that five-step sequence of central events—is at the heart of your book. Now you'll begin to see why I consider the Story Core to be so vital. It is responsible for the inverted-triangle shape of good pacing. Think about it: first you have your character—a broad idea, and the character might go off in any direction. But next, he realizes that he wants something. He picks his direction. Something stands in his way, and the walls of the triangle begin to narrow. He struggles for what he wants, and the squeeze grows tighter. And finally, he either succeeds or fails—you reach the point of the triangle.

Every single chapter in your book must have this same pattern.

At the beginning of a chapter, the character has varying options. The specific path for this chapter hasn't yet been chosen; he has choices (will he choose an action that takes him closer to fixing his flaw?). He's faced with distractions (will he deviate from his hero's journey here? Some of those distractions look pretty tempting!)

Early to midway through the chapter, the character must want something specific, and set his eyes on the prize. This goal may be related to the larger, external goal—the one that's driving the whole plot. Or it may be related to your story in a vaguer way, connected by character arc or theme.

He must come up against some sort of opposition. This doesn't need to be the book's key antagonist, but *something* makes it difficult for the character to easily achieve his immediate, in-chapter desire.

He struggles to reach his goal, and either succeeds or fails—and that success or failure is the direct cause of the next chapter. It's because the main character succeeds or fails in his immediate, in-chapter struggle that he finds himself at the start of the next chapter, at the wide end of a new triangle, faced with new choices and temptations.

The same pattern applies to scenes *within* chapters. If you like to separate your action with scene breaks (or line breaks, as my copy editor insists on calling them... darn it, she's probably correct), you need to apply the same triangular pattern to each scene.

In the overall story, your character has his external goal. In this chapter, he has a more immediate, less motivating, but still important goal. He believes (and maybe he's right) that by achieving his in-chapter goal, he'll get one step closer to achieving his external goal. In each scene within each chapter, he has an even more immediate, but still important, goal. He believes (rightly?) that by achieving his in-scene goal, he'll get one step closer to achieving his in-chapter goal, which he's pretty sure will bring him one step closer to his big, external goal.

In each chapter and scene, his goal won't come easily. He's going to have to go through at least *some* conflict to reach it. Maybe it's as simple as needing to get to the pharmacy to pick up medicine for his sick kid, but the roads are icy, so the drive will be hair-raising. In each scene within each chapter, he must face similar opposition to his in-scene goal.

Chapter goal: pick up medicine for his sick kid. Chapter opposition: the roads are icy. Scene goal: drive to the pharmacy safely despite the dangerous road conditions. Scene opposition: he hits a patch of black ice and swerves into a ditch.

You can see that chapter and scene goals/ oppositions don't need to be big, monumental things. They can be relatively insignificant. But they must be present—and they must be logical, with one naturally leading into the next, and all of them ultimately converging on the main character's big, external goal—in order to keep the reader glued to the page.

Pacing: The Cymbal Crash

It's easy to feel overwhelmed by this concept of building pace deliberately into your outline. If you've never done it before, it seems like so much *work* to figure all this stuff out, and so daunting to think up all these new goals and oppositions and struggles and outcomes.

I promise that it's worth the effort. When you put in the work *now*, in the outlining phase, you save immeasurable amounts of time *later*, in the writing phase. If you can be assured of a tight, compelling pace before you even begin writing, then it might not matter whether every other aspect of your book is well-crafted. Your dialog could be wooden and your characters shallow, your prose sophomoric and your plot events silly. *Most readers will still want to keep on reading* if you can just nail your pace.

It's mostly confidence in a logical, compelling plot—in a pace that is made of related events, with plenty of "squeeze" from the sides of the triangles—that allows me to have such confidence in my books before I begin writing, to set crazy-short deadlines for myself, and to fly through the writing process. Believe me when I say that it's *so* worth the effort of building pace into your outline.

But I have invented *another* trick to make the pace-building phase go as quickly and easily as possible. (I'm just full of tricks, and now you are, too!)

I know from experience that it can be difficult to select the right kinds of in-chapter or in-scene goals, and the right kinds of oppositions for those goals. How do you make in-scene goals feel important without overwhelming the importance of the overall struggle for the external goal?

I've found it helpful to pay special attention to the final moment in a chapter or scene—the moment when the character reaches the point of the triangle, when he is just on the verge of spilling out of his "funnel" into the wide mouth of the next logical triangle.

I call these moments "cymbal crashes." Just like a cymbal in an orchestra, these moments highlight the big, dramatic crescendos, and punctuate the climaxes of passages—just to be sure the reader doesn't miss the point of the passage. In music, you'll never find a cymbal crash in the middle of an opening passage (unless you're listening to a march.) They always come at the height of musical tension, and they send an extra little thrill up the listener's spine (and the musicians' spines. I think this is why I've always dated percussionists: all my time spent sitting in orchestra pits has given me the impression that whoever holds the cymbals is the most exciting guy in the place!)

So as I fill in my sketchy, preliminary outline, adding new in-chapter goals and conflicts for my character, I look hard at the final moment of each chapter or scene. Does it have a cymbal crash? I carefully consider the visual or emotional "last impression" of each and every scene in each and every chapter. Does the final image cause a thrill up the spine—a "Whoah!" sensation, or an "Uh-oh" or an "Ah-HA"?

If the logical outcome of that chapter's or scene's action doesn't end on a cymbal crash—if the only logical outcome feels bland and tame—I re-think the goal and opposition for that chapter/scene. By ensuring that I can logically punctuate every point of every triangle with a cymbal crash, I'm ensuring that whatever action comes before is leading to a moment of excitement, and will give the reader no opportunity to set the book aside.

Cymbal crashes can be rather subtle—maybe I should say that most of the time, they *should* be rather subtle. You don't have to beat the reader over the head with your cymbals in order to send a thrill up their spine. I'll give you an example of one short scene with two endings: one ending that lacks a subtle cymbal crash, and one that has a subtle cymbal crash.

Lucy juggled a stack of mail and her purse with one hand, and fished her apartment key out of her coat pocket with the other. It had been a long day at work—entirely too much office drama. She was looking forward to taking her dog Toby out for a walk, then unwinding with a cup of tea and a romance novel.

Just before she could climb the steps to her apartment, tires squealed in the parking lot behind her. Lucy looked around to see Mary's blue Honda Civic shuddering to a halt. Mary leaned across the passenger seat and cranked down the window.

"Lucy!" Mary called. "I really need your help!"

Reluctantly, Lucy approached the Honda. Mary was always full of drama, and Lucy'd had her fill for today. But she could see tears streaking Mary's cheeks. Maybe something was really wrong this time.

"What's the matter?" Lucy asked, bending to peer into the car.

"I think Sam is cheating on me," Mary sobbed. "Will you come with me to find out? I'm going to follow him when he leaves work to see where he's really going."

Lucy stifled a sigh. That cup of tea sounded really good, and she was sure Toby had to pee. She was tempted to say no, for fear that she'd come home to another puddle on the carpet—more work to be done, and more money lost to a pet deposit she'd never get back. But Mary looked really distraught this time. Maybe this time, the drama was real.

She stuffed her mail into her purse and opened the car's door. "Okay," she said. "I'll go with you."

Now read the ending of the same scene again, this time with a subtle cymbal crash added:

Lucy stifled a sigh. That cup of tea sounded really good, and she was sure Toby had to pee. She was tempted to say no, for fear that she'd come home to another puddle on the carpet—more work to be done, and more money lost to a pet deposit she'd never get back. But Mary looked really distraught this time. Maybe this time, the drama was real.

She stuffed her mail into her purse and opened the car's door. "Okay," she said. "I'll go with you."

As Mary wheeled the Honda around and peeled off toward the highway, Lucy glanced up at her apartment window. Toby stared back down at her. His fuzzy face looked desperate, and Lucy was sure she'd never get that pet deposit back. This time, Mary's little adventure had better produce more than just another bout of pointless drama.

In the first version, the goal and opposition are clear. They're not monumental issues, but they're there. Lucy struggles with her decision, and finally makes her choice. But the end of the scene feels dry and forgettable, because there's no cymbal crash punctuating it.

In the second version, the ending features a cymbal crash. It's nothing huge—it doesn't need to be—but it leaves the reader with a vivid visual and emotional "final image"—a sensation that Lucy's choice to help Mary really means something, and will spur further action in the book.

If you're having a hard time devising in-chapter/in-scene goals and conflicts, look to the end of the scene. If it doesn't have a cymbal crash, adding one in could make all the difference—not only in sending a tiny thrill up your reader's spine, but in revealing to you just what the in-scene conflict and opposition should be.

Pacing: Expanding the Outline

Now that you understand pacing, it's time to expand your outline into "beats"—brief descriptions of what happens in each chapter and scene.

Your beats will become your template for writing your book. Once you've got all your beats in place, each with a triangle shape that funnels into the next, you'll be ready to write your book by simply fleshing out each beat with prose.

In the beat-writing phase, I take a look at the roughly sketched outline with all of its filled-in plot headings. I think about how I'll logically move my character from one heading to the next. Let's return to Pocahontas's outline for *Tidewater* as an example.

Here are the first three plot headings in my outline:

<u>Opening Scene:</u> Preparing for a feast, she shirks her duties and angers Matachanna.

<u>Inciting Event:</u> Given as handmaid to a high-born relative; dissatisfied with her lot in life.

<u>Character Realizes External Goal:</u> Sees female chieftain arrive; clearly wants to be a chieftain herself.

In looking at these headings, I know that I need to accomplish a few key things with my beats:

1. Set the stage (in this case, preparing for a feast)

2. Make Pocahontas show her flaw by shirking her duties, thus angering Matachanna

3. See a female chieftain arrive

4. Make Pocahontas's external goal clear

5. Give her as a handmaid to a high-born relative

6. Show her dissatisfaction

You'll note that in considering my beats, I flip-flopped the order of a couple of my headings. That's okay—at this stage, give yourself the flexibility to re-order some headings if it will assist the logical flow of events.

Now, in a new document, begin creating your beats. You can number them if you like, so you'll have a clear idea of where chapter or scene breaks might fall. I like to simply create a new paragraph for each beat (and each beat will become a chapter, or a significant scene within a chapter.)

Beats for the beginning of Tidewater, *Pocahontas's portion of the story:*

Matachanna finds Pocahontas napping, even though they're supposed to be preparing for a feast. She wakes Pocahontas and scolds her for her selfishness. Pocahontas shows no remorse, proving how she got the nickname "Mischief." Matachanna forgives her—they are devoted sisters—but admonishes her to be on her best behavior today, because many chiefs are coming from all the tribes to hear their father speak on an important topic. Matachanna lends Pocahontas pearls to wear—something only high-born girls get. The pearls make Pocahontas resolve to really be good. She wants to be worthy of her sister's esteem, and worthy of the pearls. She promises she'll try her best.

All the girls and women gather on the shoreline to watch the chiefs arrive in their canoes. Even with her pearls, Pocahontas feels her low-born status keenly amidst all the finery the high-born women display. She jokes and clowns to make herself feel more important. The first tribe to arrive is Appamattuck, ruled by a rare female chief. Pocahontas's happy mood dries up at the sight of her, and Matachanna can tell by the look on Pocahontas's face that she secretly wants to be a chief, too. Matachanna quietly warns her to remember her place and to remember that she's not born to be a chief. Traveling with the female chief is a little girl, Nonoma. Pocahontas can tell from the expensive paint Nonoma wears that she is very high-born indeed. Pocahontas, as a low-born girl, is chosen to be Nonoma's servant while she's in the capital city. Pocahontas is infuriated at being cast in this role, feeling farther away from her ambitions than ever before. When they are alone, Nonoma puts on airs and treats Pocahontas like a slave. Pocahontas insults Nonoma and even spits in her face. When Nonoma collapses in tears, Pocahontas feels real remorse for her bullying, and tries to make amends by giving Nonoma her favorite hair ornament. Nonoma agrees to an uneasy truce, but Pocahontas warns her that they must try to treat each other kindly—even if Pocahontas is far below Nonoma in status.

Here you can see how I've expanded the rough sketches that accompany my plot headings. Paying heed to Pocahontas's character arc and her external goal, I've filled these two beats with details about her actions and personality, and have added the actions of some characters around her. You'll note that I've only bothered with including Matachanna's and Nonoma's actions and personalities—because it's Pocahontas's interactions with these two characters that show what kind of person my main character is at the beginning of the story.

I've accomplished everything I needed to do, according to my outline: set the stage, show Pocahontas's flaw and external goal, give her as a handmaid to her high-born relative, and show her dissatisfaction with her lot in life.

I've included my cymbal crashes—in the first beat, it's the image of Pocahontas wearing pearls for the first time; in the next beat, the cymbal crash is the moment when Pocahontas gives her favorite ornament to her "frenemy," but warns Nonoma that she expects to be treated with respect, even if she is low-born.

The in-scene goals and conflicts are clear: in the first beat, Pocahontas's goal is to give up her mischievous ways and really be a good girl, to please her sister—but she's fighting against her selfish nature, so it'll be hard. In the second scene, Pocahontas wants to be treated with respect even though she's low-born. First she clowns around to try to get attention (part of her struggle to achieve that goal) and later she bullies Nonoma.

Now, as you write your actual book, you'll be able to expand even further. The simple, focused beats will grow into a rich world full of detail, dialog, and emotion. As I wrote Pocahontas's first chapter in *Tidewater*, I certainly added in plenty of peripheral characters and all kinds of fun details that brought my main character's world to life. But since my beats were focused on Pocahontas and those who reflect her flaw—Matachanna and Nonoma—even in the midst of colorful world-building I ensured that I didn't get too sidetracked with other characters or events in the opening chapter. The purpose of the opening chapter still feels relevant—it's exploring Pocahontas's flaw, her need for change. The peripheral characters and world-building details are added here and there for color, but the real focus is on Pocahontas, Matachanna, and Nonoma, just as it is in my beats.

From here, it's a relatively simple task to expand all of your plot headings into beats. Just take it one beat at a time, envisioning a logical way to bridge the gap from one heading to the next. Always keep an eye on pace—remember that each beat should have a Story Core hidden somewhere inside, with a new (albeit minor) goal, conflict, and resolution for your character, and a cymbal crash at the end to maintain a sense of tension and importance.

By the time you get to the end of your outline, using inverted-triangle-shaped beats to bridge from one plot heading to the next, you'll have a completed outline.

But more than that: you'll have an outline that guarantees your book will be compelling and interesting, with a solid character arc that leaves the reader feeling satisfied, glad they've spent time with your book. Because you've put in the time up-front to ensure a well-paced, logical plot, and because you've only included scenes which bear directly on character arc, Story Core, and theme, you can feel assured that you'll use your writing time as efficiently as possible—that you won't waste days or weeks (months?) writing yourself into a corner, only to delete all that work later on.

You've done it! You've outlined a book with

complete assurance that it will be a good one, and now you're ready to write.

Doesn't it feel great to take off your pants?

Outlining Multi-Main-Character Books

Now you have a thorough understanding of how to outline a book with *one* main character. But what do you do for books with more than one central character? Some books, like romances, virtually always have two main characters of equal importance—sometime they have more than two! Other books, like my own *Tidewater*, utilize multiple central characters as a way of exploring the book's theme from a variety of angles.

Any main character—anyone who goes on a hero's journey, struggling to conquer his flaw and emerge after the climax as a better person—will need a complete character arc. And you know by now how to create a complete character arc, and how to support it with a plot.

Therefore, in multi-main-character books like *Tidewater*, you'll need to make a complete outline for each main character.

But how do you know whether your characters are *really* main? Are they truly sharing the protagonist spotlight, or do they play other important roles in the narrative, such as antagonist or ally?

Often, point-of-view characters who get to control a portion of the narrative voice are main characters. Not *always*—but often. If they frequently enjoy the POV spotlight, they're probably protagonists, and not supporting cast.

POV is a fairly reliable rule of thumb, but it's not always accurate, and it only applies to first- or third-person perspectives. What about omniscient perspective? An omniscient narrator is not one of the "players" involved in the action of the book, yet it has an individual voice and is a character of sorts—a distinct personality. The entire story is told from the narrator's POV, not from the POV of any character who's involved with the story in a material way.

But even relying on POV alone for first- and third-person narration can trip you up. Sometimes a narrating character who's involved in the plot is really there to observe and report on the true protagonist's character arc. The best example here is Dr. Watson in the *Sherlock Holmes* stories. Watson always narrates, and he nearly always plays the ally role, but he virtually never gets a character arc of his own. His purpose as narrator is to convey

Holmes's hero-journey to the reader.

The very best yardstick for determining a main character is the presence of a serious flaw. Does this character have an inner problem that's impacting his life or the lives of the people he loves? Then he's in need of a hero's journey: let's give him an outline!

In *Tidewater*, Matachanna plays a large part in the story from start to finish. But she doesn't have any truly serious flaw. Matachanna's got it all together; she knows how to get along with others, and she has a balanced, effective approach to tackling life's problems. She's important to the story, but she isn't in need of a change. Therefore, I had no reason to give her a complete arc with an outline.

But *Tidewater* does have two other main characters. John Smith, the English settler, is a cynical person whose bitterness makes him treat other people with contempt—and ultimately holds him back from achieving his goals. He's clearly in need of change, so *Tidewater* is just as much an exploration of his hero-journey as Pocahontas's. Opechancanough, the uncle of Pocahontas, is a man whose quick temper has held him back many times before. His rage gets the better of him, and he doesn't always make the best decisions. He's in need of real growth before he can become the wise leader he wants to be. Together, these three characters allow me to use an intriguing unifying theme for

Tidewater: an exploration of three potential ways a person might respond to a cultural clash.

And I find *that* the very best way to ensure that I'm including relevant multiple protagonists in my books: make them relate clearly to the book's theme. Flaws are all well and good on their own, but if each main character's flaw isn't some exploration of a unifying theme, you run the risk of making the reader feel as if she's reading two stories at once. Determine main-character status by evaluating flaw first, then theme... but don't neglect to check your character's flaw against the book's unifying theme.

Once you've determined that you do indeed have multiple protagonists, work through their outline as you would for a single-main-character book. But bear in mind that in multi-main-character books, your main characters often become antagonists to one another. Often, they're all pursuing the same external goal, or their external goals are so closely related that only one of them can win his individual goal, and if he wins, the others will lose their struggles.

That's okay—it's quite natural, actually, for multiple main characters to act as one another's antagonists (in fact, this is a very common device in the romance genre.) Just work through one outline at a time, treating each character's arc with equal care. It's okay if John Smith is a main character, but *also* the antagonist of Opechancanough. Keep the focus of John Smith's outline on *his* goals, both external and internal, and worry about Opechancanough's goals when it's time to write his outline.

If you're sure you've got a multi-main-character book, complete the outline process up through the "sketch in plot headings" phase, and push on to write beats for each character's first one or two scenes. This will give you a clear idea of how each character's storyline will be established.

When you have all your plot points sketched in and when you know the details of how each character's arc will be introduced, it's time to begin weaving your multiple outlines together.

This is much simpler than you might be picturing. You have each character's plot points set up, in loose terms. Now you simply have to *look for opportunities for your characters to meet.*

What logical string of events—what series of inverted triangles—will lead Pocahontas into contact with John Smith? Bear in mind that multiple main characters are usually one another's antagonists, so pay special attention to how you'll maneuver each character to the *conflict points*, where they will vie with one another for their external goals. Write beats that will move your characters toward their meeting points or conflict points.

Now and then you'll need to leave off one main character's storyline for a while, in order to take up another's and develop *his* logical chain of events, leading inevitably to the next conflict between *both* main characters. When you drop one character's storyline, be sure to deliver an extra-big cymbal crash at the point where you let it go. Cliffhangers can work well here, but they're not necessary. A dramatic image that really speaks to the book's theme *is* necessary. That way, even though you're leaving Pocahontas's storyline to follow John Smith's, the reader still feels that Pocahontas's story is important, and the decision to watch John develop his character feels intrinsically related to Pocahontas. A big cymbal crash helps assure the reader that you're not just trailing off pointlessly, losing interest with the first character and moving along to another who has nothing to do with the story.

Continue trading back and forth between your main characters as often as you feel is necessary, filling out their beats to bridge the gaps between their individual plot headings. Don't feel like you must switch rhythmically between one main character and the other. Sometimes that works out great, but it's not always the best way to pace a book.

Commit to switching between your main characters only when you can give the reader a really loud cymbal crash—when one character's storyline has built up to a really dramatic "Whoah!" moment. *Then* you can change gears, and take up the storyline of your next main character. This might mean that you stick with one character for a long time—several chapters, or maybe half the book! That's okay. Let the drama and tension of your pace be your guide. Those trickly little inverted triangles will never steer you wrong.

In multi-main-character works—especially very long ones, like six-figure-wordcount tomes or multi-volume epics—some main characters may drop out of the plot at one point or another. If they reach the natural end of their character arc long before your other protagonists do, don't sweat it. They may lose their goal (but learn their personal lesson) early in the book; they may die heroically trying to achieve their goal. It's all right. As long as you still have one protagonist and one antagonist locked in a struggle, your story is still going, even if all the rest of your protagonists are no longer in the picture. Don't feel like you must make each character's arc end at the same climax. Remember that each character is the hero of his own story, and as far as *he's* concerned, his story has little to do with anybody else's. Strike each of his plot points, including his battle, "death," and outcome, where they feel most logical and natural. Don't try to prolong any character's arc artificially.

What About Series?

I've received a lot of questions since first publishing *Take Off Your Pants!*, but the most common question has certainly been how one handles a character's arc over the course of a series.

There's really no right or wrong way to approach a character's arc within a series. Under my two active pen names (as of October, 2015) I've written four series, and I've handled character arcs a little bit differently in each one. You can choose whichever method works best for your particular story and your character's special journey.

One way to apply character arc over a long series is to allow the arc to build slowly over the course of multiple volumes. In the *Harry Potter* books, Harry's inner goal is to grow into the leader he's destined to be. He tries hard in each volume—and each time, he gets a little bit closer. But he never quite achieves full hero status until the end of the final book, when he reaches the grand climax of the series.

J.K. Rowling pushes Harry closer to fixing his flaw with each book, but never quite gets him there until the last installment. That's a perfectly valid approach to take, and obviously it can create gripping series that fans adore! You can see the same "getting closer, but not there yet" strategy in *A Song of Ice and Fire* by George R. R. Martin, Veronica Roth's *Divergent* series, and *The Righteous* series by Michael Wallace.

There's also an entirely different method of plotting a multi-book series that features the same character(s). You can allow your character to resolve her initial flaw by the end of Book 1, but give her a whole new flaw to tackle in Book 2. As long as the new flaw is derived from the events that took place in Book 1, it will feel relevant and coherent. Your character must go on a whole new hero's journey, but the new flaw—and thus the new journey—has grown organically out of the trials your character has already faced.

Find examples of this type of flaw-solution-flaw pattern in *The Hunger Games* trilogy by Suzanne Collins, the *Twilight Saga* by Stephenie Meyer, and Robert Ludlum's *Jason Bourne* series.

Another means of handling multi-book/same-character series can be observed in popular thriller and cozy mystery books. Your character might struggle to overcome the *same* flaw in every book. This happens frequently in genres where readers key into comforting familiarity and appreciate endearingly quirky traits in their main characters. Think of Stephanie Plum in Janet Evanovich's long-running series. Stephanie's ditzy approach to life holds her back until she manages to wise up long enough to solve each mystery... but she's back to being the same old Stephanie by the start of the next book.

That's an acceptable approach to take with any series—and you'll also find it used in other long-running, mystery- and action-themed franchises like *James Bond*, *Sherlock Holmes*, and many of the *Star Trek* novels. It won't work for every type of series or for every audience, but with the right audience it lights up all the right signals and keeps your target readers coming back for more.

To Be Pants-Free

Now you know the secret to unlocking speed and confidence in your writing—to setting and meeting tight writing deadlines, and efficiently producing books that are guaranteed to delight your readers. Assurance in a new book's quality—even *before* you start writing—is only an outline away.

I know the process seems daunting, especially if you've never tried to outline a book before. But like any other very simple skill, all it takes is a small amount of practice, and you can master it with ease.

My outlining process seems very long and involved when it's written out in this didactic form. But on average, after having written the outlines for more than twenty novels (including a few multi-main-character books, which take much more planning and thought) it takes me about four hours to complete an outline.

Four hours (or less, for simpler plots) is a very manageable time investment, since you can be sure that this method will save you goodness-knows-how-many hours compared to "flying by the seat of your pants"!

When you're contemplating ways to tackle your next book, give my outlining method a try. I think you'll be pleased with the confidence it instills, and I know you'll love how quickly and easily a good book comes together for you.

I'm sure you'll be glad that you took off your pants after all.

ACKNOWLEDGMENTS

Big thanks to my friends and fellow authors, who provided feedback on an early draft of this book: Nathan Lowell, Cidney Swanson, and Krista Ball. I appreciate the assistance and the enthusiasm for learning my personal take on this sometimes controversial topic (controversial among writers, anyway.)

Thanks to all those who bought my first how-to book for authors, *Gotta Read It! Five Simple Steps to a Fiction Pitch That Sells*. The interest in my first how-to work assured me that there was a market for more. I hope you all find this book useful.

MORE BOOKS BY LIBBIE HAWKER

How-To Books for Authors:

Gotta Read It! Five Simple Steps to a Fiction Pitch That Sells

How to Write Historical Fiction That Sells (Fall, 2015)

A Ringing Gong: Writing By Ear for Memorable Prose (forthcoming)

The Only Rule: Busting the Myths of Ficiton Writing (forthcoming)

Fiction:

The Sekhmet Bed (The She-King, Book 1)

The Crook and Flail (The She-King, Book 2)

Sovereign of Stars (The She-King, Book 3)

The Bull of Min (The She-King, Book 4)

Tidewater

Baptism for the Dead

House of Rejoicing

Storm in the Sky

Eater of Hearts (March, 2016)

Daughter of Sand and Stone (From Lake Union Publishing, Dec. 1, 2015)

Mercer Girls (From Lake Union Publishing, June 2016)

ABOUT THE AUTHOR

Libbie Hawker is an independent author who has written nearly twenty novels under two different pen names. Once fervently in pursuit of the dream agent and "proper" traditional publishing contracts, she quickly shifted her focus after she self-published her first novel, *The Sekhmet Bed*, and watched as its sales outstripped those of many traditionally published historical novels. Now she advocates for self-publishing, and although she began a partnership with Lake Union in late 2014, she continues to independently publish the majority of her works.

Libbie's books feature complex characters and rich details of time and place. Find more information at LibbieHawker.com.